T0317957

WAINWRIGHT'S

COAST TO COAST WALK

WALKERS EDITION

View from South Head, St. Bees, looking to Black Combe

A
COAST TO COAST
WALK

(ST. BEES HEAD to ROBIN HOOD'S BAY)

WALKERS EDITION

REVISED BY CHRIS JESTY

A PICTORIAL GUIDE

AWainwright

THIS REVISED AND UPDATED
EDITION FOR WALKERS
PUBLISHED BY
FRANCES LINCOLN
LONDON

Wainwright's Coast to Coast Walk

Text and illustrations © The Estate of
A. Wainwright 1973, 2003, 2010

Revisions and additional material © Chris Jesty 2010, 2014
Cover photograph © Karen Frenkel 2017

First published in 1973 by the Westmorland
Gazette, Kendal; updated, 1994, 1995, 1998, 2003
First published by Frances Lincoln Ltd in 2003
Second (revised) edition published in 2010
Reprinted with minor corrections 2014
'Walkers Edition' published in 2017

Frances Lincoln,
an imprint of the Quarto Group,
The Old Brewery, 6 Blundell Street, London N7 9BH
www.Quarto.com

Printed and bound in the United Kingdom.

A CIP catalogue record is available for this book
from the British Library

ISBN 978 0 7112 3919 7

2 4 6 8 9 7 5 3 1

Dedicated to

THE SECOND PERSON
TO WALK FROM
ST. BEES HEAD
TO ROBIN HOOD'S BAY

INTRODUCTION TO THE SECOND EDITION

Although changes have been made since this book was originally published, this is the first time that every word of text and every feature on the maps has been brought up to date. In this edition the route is shown in red on the maps to distinguish it from off-route paths and other detail, and in one section alternative paths are shown in blue and green. No changes have been made to Wainwright's personal notes in conclusion or to the illustrations (except for the drawing on page 85, which was taken from *A Second Dales Sketchbook* to fill the space).

In my opinion the best part of the route is the final quarter of a mile through the village of Robin Hood's Bay, and time should be allowed for the exploration of every lane. The second best place is the Forces on Measand Beck on page 53. To see the finest of the waterfalls you have to follow the beck upstream for about 200 yards.

I should like to thank Andy Robinson, Bob Watson and David Moreton for drawing my attention to errors, which have now been corrected.

Chris Jesty
Kendal, March 2014

CONTENTS

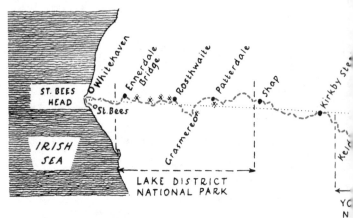

ALTITUDES

(Vertical scale greatly exaggerated)

The highest point reached is Kidsty Pike, 256[0]

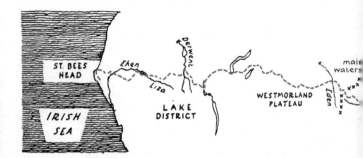

THE ROUTE

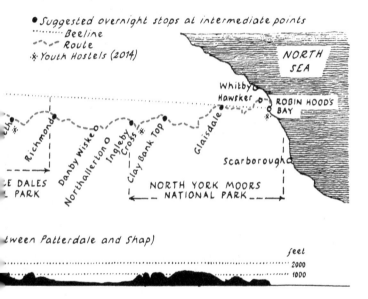

- Suggested overnight stops at intermediate points
.... Beeline
--- Route
❋ Youth Hostels (2014)

NORTH SEA

Whitby
Hawsker
ROBIN HOOD'S BAY

Richmond
Danby Wiske
Northallerton
Ingleby Cross
Clay Bank Top
Glaisdale
Scarborough

DALES PARK

NORTH YORK MOORS NATIONAL PARK

(between Patterdale and Shap)

feet
2000
1000

NATURAL FEATURES

--- Route
〜 Rivers

VALE OF MOWBRAY
CLEVELAND HILLS
Esk
ROBIN HOOD'S BAY

NORTH YORK MOORS

NORTH SEA

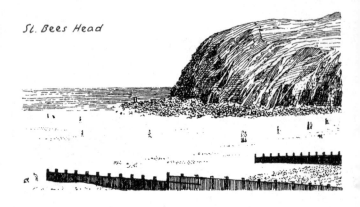

St. Bees Head

INTRODUCTION

Every walker who plans a cross-country expedition refers to his maps, looks for the footpaths and the bridleways and the areas of open access, links them together by quiet roads and lanes that avoid towns and busy traffic arteries, and so devises a pleasant route to his objective that he is free to walk, as is any man, without fear of trespass or restriction.

This is precisely what I have done in the book. To the best of my knowledge the route described will commit no offence against privacy nor trample on the sensitive corns of landowners and tenants. It is a country walk of the sort that enthusiasts for the hills and open spaces indulge in every weekend. It's a bit longer than most, that's all.

The point I want to emphasise is that the route herein described is in no sense an "official route" such as the Pennine Way — it has not needed the approval of the Countryside Commission or indeed any other body nor have any permissions needed to be sought. It is a harmless and enjoyable walk across England, entirely (so far as I am aware) on existing rights of way or over ground where access is traditionally free to all.

The walk is one I have long had in mind, and in 1972 finally accomplished; and I have committed it to print partly because the growing popularity of the Pennine Way indicates that many people of all ages welcome the challenge of a long-distance walk, and partly because I want to encourage in others the ambition to devise with the aid of maps their own cross-country marathons and not be merely followers of other people's routes: there is no end to the possibilities for originality and initiative. And partly, I suppose, because I like to write about my walks and by doing so live them over again.

Pillar,
Lake District

One should always have a definite objective, in a walk as in life — it is so much more satisfying to reach a target by personal effort than to wander aimlessly.   An objective is an ambition, and life without ambition is ..... well, aimless wandering.
The objective in this book is Robin Hood's Bay, on the Yorkshire coast: doubly satisfying because it is not only an attractive place to finish a walk (ice cream, girls and all that — oh, and scenery) but also very definitive: here land ends and sea begins. You can't walk on water, and Robin Hood's Bay is a definite full stop, a terminus absolute.

The route follows an approximate beeline (if a beeline can ever be approximate!) from one side of England to the other: from St. Bees Head on the Irish Sea to Robin Hood's Bay on the North Sea and if a ruler is placed across a map between these two points it will be seen at a glance that the grandest territory in the north of England is traversed by it; indeed, two-thirds of the route lies through the areas of three National Parks.

The walk commences on the sea-cliffs of St. Bees Head, passes through the heart of Lakeland, and crosses the Westmorland limestone plateau, the Eden Valley and the Pennine watershed, whence it accompanies Swaledale and then aims across the Vale of Mowbray to the Cleveland Hills and North York Moors to end on the sea-cliffs of Robin Hood's Bay.

Surely there cannot be a finer itinerary for a long-distance walk! For sustained beauty, variety and interest it puts the Pennine Way to shame.

On the Cleveland Hills

It is never possible to follow a dead-straight beeline over a long distance without trespassing: climbing fences, wading rivers, perhaps swimming sheets of water, and walking through houses and gardens. In fact, no straight line on a map will give a dead-straight beeline because it is now generally accepted in the best circles that the earth is round, not flat, and a straight line on a map must therefore be incorrect to the extent of the curvature between the two points, however slight. The route given in this book makes no attempt to follow a straight line: deviations are necessary throughout, primarily to avoid private ground but additionally to take the opportunity of visiting places of special interest nearby — without ever losing sight of the final objective. Thus although the straight line gives a mileage of 125, the route mileage is 190: half as far again.

The Old Gang Mines near Swaledale

The countryside traversed is beautiful almost everywhere, yet extremely varied in character, with mountains and hills, valleys and rivers, heather moors and sea cliffs combining in a pageant of colourful scenery. It is of great interest both topographically and geologically, the structure of the terrain and the formations of the rocks showing marked changes from one district to the next. Evidences in plenty are met of prehistoric and early British settlements, while many abandoned mineral workings dating from medieval times offer a fascinating study for the industrial archaeologist. You see part of the history of England on this walk.

The route, which has a bias in favour of high ground rather than low, is divided into convenient sections, each of sufficient distance to provide a good day's march for the average walker and ending at a place where overnight lodgings are normally available. In some of the villages accommodation is scarce and in summer particularly it eases the mind during the day to know that a bed for the night is assured. Yet it is unwise to book too far ahead in advance: bad weather may prohibit progress as planned and play havoc with a pre-arranged programme, and it is better to book ahead after breakfast, each morning, by telephone, only if the weather is favourable. Youth hostellers are well served, most of the way, but on some nights must seek other accommodation or sleep under the stars.

Given reasonable weather, the walk can be done in two weeks, not rushing it nor trailing behind schedule. A very strong athlete might do it in a week, but this is a walk that ought to be done in comfort and for pleasure or not at all.

Some readers who would like to do the walk may, for a variety of reasons, prefer to tackle the sections at intervals of time and possibly not in sequence, travelling from home on each occasion: this practice has other advantages, notably avoidance of the need to reserve a bed and the selection of fine clear days only, while leaving you free to go to Majorca for your main holiday if your wife keeps on nagging about it. Everybody has a car these days, even me (and, in my case, a good-looking, competent chauffeur to go with it) and most sections of the route are within reach of the urban areas in the northern counties. The route detailed in this book is my own preference, but some walkers may choose to vary it in places, either to make additional detours or to short-cut corners, or even follow their own course over lengthy distances. Such personal initiatives are to be encouraged — if they do not involve trespass. The way you go and the time it takes matter not. The essence of the walk is the crossing of England, from one coast to the other, on foot.

The walk is described from west to east. It is generally better in this country to walk from the west or south so as to have the weather on your back and not in your face. In the case of this particular walk it is perhaps unfortunate that the grandest part of it, through Lakeland, comes so early, but those who do not already know the heather moors of north-east Yorkshire can be assured that they form a fitting climax.

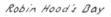

Robin Hood's Bay

THE SECTIONS
OF THE ROUTE

SECTION MAP : *ST. BEES to ENNERDALE BRIDGE* : 14¼ miles

IRISH SEA

Whitehaven

A5086

Ennerdale Bridge

Sandwith

Cleator Moor

ST. BEES HEAD

A595

Cleator

RHB

DENT

St. Bees

START

Egremont

Detailed maps and narrative — on pages 1–11

St. Bees

Saint Bees (always abbreviated to St. Bees) is an ancient community with deep-rooted ecclesiastical and scholastic foundations. Here was established a nunnery in the 7th century by St. Bega, this being succeeded on the site by a Benedictine Priory in the 12th century. After the dissolution of the monasteries the Priory, then ruinous, was restored and adopted as the present Parish Church under the name of the Priory Church of St. Mary and St. Bega. The original fabric has largely been superseded in the course of later alteration and repair but some interesting features remain, notably the west doorway, erected in 1150: a splendid example of Norman architecture.

The Grammar School, known nationally, was founded in 1583 by the then Archbishop of Canterbury under a charter granted by Queen Elizabeth I. It is set around an elegant quadrangle opposite the Church, both buildings being constructed of the red sandstone so much in evidence locally.

The village straddles the sheltered valley of Pow Beck through which runs the main railway serving the towns of west Cumbria. The coast, half a mile away, is the modern attraction with its extensive sands beyond a massive concrete seawall, built in 1959-61 to prevent erosion, and wide areas of colourful boulders, some of them fallen from the cliffs, others deposited here from the inland mountains by the retreating glaciers long ago.

The west doorway, Priory Church.

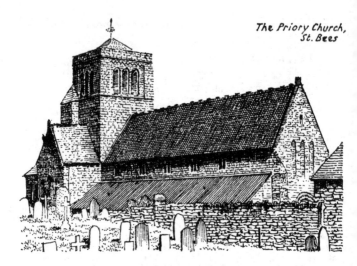

*The Priory Church,
St. Bees*

St. Bees Head

North of the foreshore at St. Bees rises the lofty bulwark of
St. Bees Head, four miles of towering and precipitous cliffs of
red sandstone veined with white, the haunt and nesting place
of countless seabirds and a rich habitat of flowers, the whole
making a gay and colourful scene, especially in springtime.

There are two main headlands, North Head and South Head, at
an average height of 300 feet, divided near Fleswick Bay by a
rocky gully. A lighthouse and a coastguard station testify to
the shipping hazards in these waters.

It is along the top of the cliffs, in the company of a continuous
wire fence, that this long journey to Robin Hood's Bay begins.

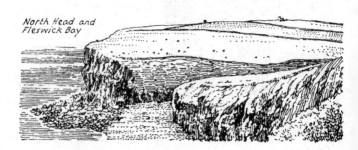

*North Head and
Fleswick Bay*

ST. BEES to SOUTH HEAD

The walk starts from the sea wall. Rather disconcertingly (because we are supposed to be heading due EAST across England to the Yorkshire coast) it aims WEST, following the cliff, soon changing course to the north. A continuous fence along the rim of the cliff, with kissing gates, is a sure guide — there is no possibility of getting lost but there is a risk of accident on the seaward side of the fence: assurance of ultimately arriving at Robin Hood's Bay is much greater if the landward side is preferred. The walk is straightforward and easy, with superb views in retrospect and exciting peeps down to the sea 300 feet below.

There are a few other features of interest:

• Pattering Holes, enclosed by a fence, is a curious fissure with conflicting legends about its origin.

• The observation point, formerly a coastguard look-out, has metal plaques describing the views to north, west and south. There are two more observation points on North Head; the first of these has paintings of birds that you are likely to see in this area.

• A prominent column 120 yards inland from the observation point holds promise of a runic cross but a visit reveals the truth — it is merely a scratching post for sheep.

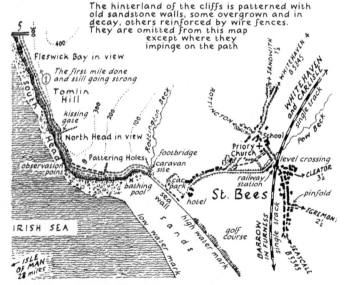

The hinterland of the cliffs is patterned with old sandstone walls, some overgrown and in decay, others reinforced by wire fences. They are omitted from this map except where they impinge on the path

On the roads into St Bees from the north-east, east and south-east there are signs saying START OF COAST TO COAST WALK, and there is a Coast to Coast Bar in the village.

North Head

St. Bees Lighthouse

The lighthouse occupies an exposed site 150 yards inland from the cliffs of the North Head at an altitude of 310 feet. It is a white-painted structure with keepers' cottages and outbuildings adjoining. The first lighthouse here was established in 1717 but was destroyed by fire and replaced in 1822. The present structure dates from 1866 and was automated in 1987. Its light is visible at sea for 25 miles.

Saltom Bay
from North Head

A: Whitehaven
B: Kells (suburb of A)
C: Chemical works
   (now gone)

SOUTH HEAD to SANDWITH

Fleswick Bay, the most beautiful part of the coast, will not be passed unnoticed. A great gash in the cliffs requires a steep descent to sea level (on a well-worn path) and a steep ascent out. By detouring inland a short way this loss and recovery of height could be avoided, but DO go down to the beach to see the splendid rock scenery, caves, pebbles, and hanging gardens of flowers.

Then proceed by the fence to the lighthouse. From here a private road (walkers have a right of way) goes to Sandwith but instead of using it continue along the cliff-top, which soon turns east to disclose a fine view of Saltom Bay and Whitehaven, with Criffell and the hills of Galloway beyond across the Solway Firth. Keep on by the fence, the path here being mostly on the seaward side, to the great crater of a working quarry, where pass round two cottages into a lane sunken between green banks. At the foot of the lane turn left into the private road going down to Sandwith, a pleasant village, with a public house but no church. Turn left here.

Anhydrite mines for the former chemical works penetrate far under St. Bees Head.

'Sandwith', is pronounced 'Sanith'
'Fleswick', is pronounced 'Flezzick'

St. Bees Head is a nature reserve of the Royal Society for the Protection of Birds. This is the only nesting site of black guillemots in England.

It is galling to find on arrival at Sandwith after walking five miles that St. Bees is less than two miles distant and that you are actually further west of Robin Hood's Bay than at the start. Never mind. St. Bees Head was well worth the detour and now so at Sandwith you can face east and march towards it with resolution.

In the event of an afternoon start from St. Bees it should be noted that there is no accommodation in Sandwith, but there is a camping barn at Tarn Flatt Hall.

The disused railways

Winding like a snake across the map on the opposite page is the line of the old railway that ran from Whitehaven to Egremont. In the 1970s it was still in use as a goods line. By the 1990s it had been transformed into the Whitehaven to Ennerdale Cycleway and the Egremont Extension, and in the first decade of the twenty-first century it became Route 72 of the National Cycle Network. The former railway from Moor Row to Rowrah is now Route 71 of the network, and Route 1 will be encountered at the other end of the Coast to Coast Walk, running from High Hawsker to Robin Hood's Bay. There are many other disused railways in the area, most of them leading to long-abandoned iron or coal mines. The cycleway is level and has an excellent tarmac surface, in contrast to the route from Stanley Pond to Scalegill Hall. The platform of Moor Row Station can still be seen, and a number of aluminium sculptures adjoin the path. Note also the mounting blocks for riders where the path crosses an unmetalled road a quarter of a mile past Moor Row Station.

The original route crossed the railway immediately to the west of Stanley Pond. It was diverted to the south at the request of British Rail.

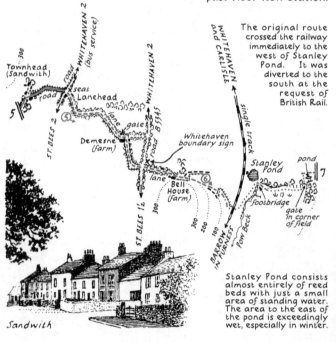

Stanley Pond consists almost entirely of reed beds with just a small area of standing water. The area to the east of the pond is exceedingly wet, especially in winter.

Sandwith

Leaving Sandwith the road rises in a curve to Lanehead, with a view ahead to the green hill of Dent and the lofty mountains beyond. At Lanehead continue on the lane facing to the farm of Demesne, where pass through the yard, turning right to reach the Whitehaven – St. Bees road. Cross it and go along the lane opposite, passing Bell House on the right. Ignore a track to the left, but when the track divides in the next field take the left fork, which leads to a pair of gates. Go through the right-hand gate and follow the right-hand side of a fence to the main-line railway. Pass under the railway and cut across the field ahead to a fence. Follow this to the left, and continue along the side of a hedge to the field corner, where there is a footbridge on the right.

Cross over it and proceed to the top of the next pasture where a gate in the left corner admits to a cart track going uphill under a railway bridge (last view here of St. Bees, still only two miles away!!) to reach the busy main road A595. Scurry across it to the road opposite, passing first the name 'MOOR ROW' spelled out in miniature hedges, and then a sculpture entitled 'Coast to Coast', created by Colin Telfer in 2007, and a milestone giving the distances to St. Bees and Robin Hood's Bay. Soon after crossing the former railway take a path on the left which joins the Whitehaven to Ennerdale Cycle Path. In half a mile turn right and immediately left at a sign saying 'Hadrian's Cycleway'. After a further half-mile bear left onto a gravel path and left again, passing between stone gateposts. A well-made path leads pleasantly into Church Street, Cleator, passing on its way a sign saying 'Wainwright's Passage'.

At Cleator there is an opportunity to interrupt the walk in case of emergency (including weary limbs) by taking a bus to Egremont nearby for an overnight stay: several hotels and bed and breakfast places – and a castle ruin. Chip shops, too.

Cleator

Cleator ("the outlying pasture among the rocks") is an old village that expanded with the boom in 19th-century iron-ore mining and in so doing sacrificed its charm and character. Some architectural pretensions are evident in its places of worship and a few older houses but completely absent in the long terraces of small cottages built to a common pattern to provide for the rapid influx of miners. Brave attempts are being made to improve these dwellings but it needs more than can come out of a tin of paint to make them attractive visually. The mines have closed; the homes of their workers remain amongst the scars as cheerless monuments to a brief prosperity that withered and died. Other mining communities nearby are similarly afflicted. Cleator Moor, a mile to the north, is a newer and larger village directly attrributable to industrial development.

There are two hotels between Cleator and Cleator Moor, one of which has three stars, but these villages make no claim to be holiday resorts or tourist centres. The primary concern of the inhabitants is to earn a living for themselves, not to cater for the leisure of others.

St. Leonard's Church

The Parish Church of Cleator, dedicated to St. Leonard, appears at first glance to be a modern building of red sandstone, but in fact the structure contains masonry dating from the 12th century, when an earlier church stood on this site, and remains of even more ancient walls found here suggest the possibility of a pre-Norman church.

The view from Dent

The green hill of Dent, once partly a deer park, is an excellent viewpoint, with a panorama far wider than its modest elevation would suggest. The whole of the west Cumbrian coastal plain from Black Combe to the Solway is seen without interruption, dotted with towns and villages as on a map.   The Isle of Man is fully in view, looking surprisingly near, and if visibility is really good it is possible to see Slieve Donard in the Mountains of Mourne over the right-hand end of the island.   But on the ascent from the west it is the sudden revelation of the Lakeland fells that rivets the attention, the prospect being unexpectedly good and ranging clockwise from the Loweswater Fells (overtopped by Skiddaw and Grasmoor) to the High Stile and Pillar groups enclosing Ennerdale, and then, best of all, a fine silhouette of Scafell Pike and Scafell. The only lake in view is Ennerdale Water, not seen to full extent.

The summit of Dent

Church Street leads into the main thoroughfare of Cleator, a busy road with a bus service. Turn left along it and, without wasting time looking for something to eat, in 60 yards go down a side-street on the right ('Kiln Brow') turning right at the bottom of the hill to Blackhow Bridge on the River Ehen (on its way from Ennerdale Water). A lane now ascends gently to the farm of Black How on a quiet byroad. Here a double gate on the roadside opposite the farmhouse gives access to a forest road climbing the fell. In a quarter of a mile turn left at a signpost to Dent Fell, and then right at a second signpost. The path eventually leaves the plantation at a stile, and oh boy does it feel good to be in open hill country with the industrial belt left behind! There follows a simple and straightforward climb alongside a crumbled wall reinforced by a wire fence to the cairn on the summit of Dent. After a good look round, continue in the same direction, crossing a broken wall to the east ridge of Dent.

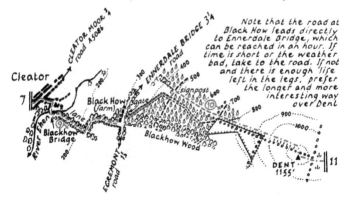

Note that the road at Black How leads directly to Ennerdale Bridge, which can be reached in an hour. If time is short or the weather bad, take to the road. If not and there is enough life left in the legs, prefer the longer and more interesting way over Dent

Raven Crag

Nannycatch

Who outside west Cumbria ever heard of Nannycatch? Yet it is within the boundary of the Lake District National Park, and a charming place — a shyly-hidden ravine continuing the much afforested valley of Uldale to the north.

A lovely beckside path runs along this Arcadia-in-miniature beneath the cliffs of Raven Crag.

Kinniside Stone Circle

According to latest information, the Kinniside Stone Circle is a bogus one, which accounts for its omission from Ordnance maps. The story (recounted in earlier books by the author and taken from a source believed to be reputable) that the circle was restored some 50 years ago after the stones had been removed by local farmers, is now regarded as a fib, the true fact being that the stones were arranged on the site merely as an example of a prehistoric circle, by a local archaeologist

Ennerdale Bridge

Ennerdale Bridge is a convenient halting place at the end of the first day. It is a quiet hamlet, known to west Cumbrians but not to the general Lakes tourist. Nevertheless a choice of lodging is to be found in or around the village, including hotels and bed-and-breakfast accommodation. There is also a bunk house at Low Cock How. *(Turn left 300 yards north of Kinniside Stone Circle.)*

DENT to ENNERDALE BRIDGE

As Ennerdale Bridge is approached, an exciting array of impressive mountains comes into view to the east, encircling the long deep valley of Ennerdale.

Now we really are on the threshold of Lakeland.....

Ennerdale Bridge

As the east ridge of Dent declines, a view of Uldale opens up ahead, attractive in spite of its dark forests of conifers, many of which have been felled. After crossing a fence go straight on at a cross-ways near a pair of water tanks and bear left onto a forest road. In fifty yards use a tall step-stile on the right to reach the open fellside again, following a path along the ridge and down to the valley on the right, and then proceeding upstream below Raven Crag. This is a delightful spot for a siesta (beware of pony-trekkers). Continue up the narrowing valley of Nannycatch Beck inclining right at its head to join the motor road from Calder Bridge roughly at the site of the Kinniside Stone Circle. Inspect this (free) and then, with the sun now low in the west, go down the road to Ennerdale Bridge and hope to secure a night's lodging. Tomorrow, Lakeland!

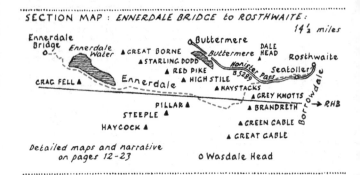

SECTION MAP : *ENNERDALE BRIDGE to ROSTHWAITE:*

14½ miles

Detailed maps and narrative on pages 12-23

o Wasdale Head

Ennerdale Water

Ennerdale Water, most westerly of the lakes, is remote from the usual haunts of Lakeland's visitors, yet it lies in a pleasantly rural setting at the outlet of a valley deeply inurned between lofty mountain ranges of which the view across the water is splendid, and in evening sunlight supremely beautiful. There is a charming pedestrian causeway along the north shore to Bowness Point and a rougher path along the south shore. The lake, renowned as a fishery for brown trout and char, unobtrusively supplies water to the people of west Cumbria.   Forty years ago a plan to raise the level of the lake by a few feet led to the premature demolition of the Anglers' Hotel, which occupied a site at the water's edge (you could fish from its window). In the event, plans to raise the water level were never implemented. The area is now managed by the Forestry Commission, the National Trust and United Utilities as part of the Wild Ennerdale initiative with the avowed aim of allowing the valley to return to a wilder state.

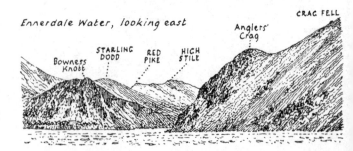

Ennerdale Water, looking east

Pillar, from Ennerdale Water

There are three Youth Hostels on the section to Borrowdale, but otherwise there is no accommodation until Seatoller is reached, and no hope of refreshment before Honister. The walking, however, is easy, with no difficulties of route-finding even in bad weather.

Leave Ennerdale Bridge by the Croasdale road, turning right in half a mile on a side-road to a bridge over the River Ehen. Go through the car park and continue to the lakeside, which then follow to the right, through a gate, to the promontory of Anglers' Crag. Keep an eye on the pinnacles high above the path.

The steep cliffs of Anglers' Crag relent a little just above water level and form a small grassy headland with low rocks. Old maps show this as Robin Hood's Chair, a name that is now in use on Ordnance Survey maps (a happy revival given its affinity with our ultimate objective: his Bay).

Robin Hood's Chair

The rough ground by the lake at the foot of Anglers' Crag was once considered impracticable for pedestrians, but in recent years booted walkers have smoothed the passage and created a track that has a little simple scrambling but no difficulties. Then follows a straightforward walk along the lakeside, paved in places, to the head of the lake, where a green path along the side of a wall is taken, cutting across a bend in the wall.

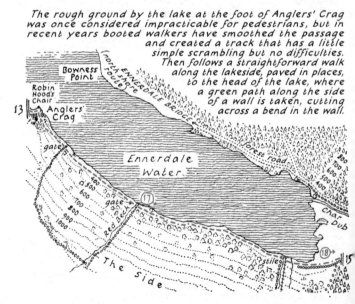

looking up Ennerdale
from the footbridge

THE HIGH STILE ALTERNATIVE:

Beyond High Gillerthwaite a delectable alternative route
is available in clear weather (only) for very strong and
experienced fellwalkers (only):
350 yards east of High Gillerthwaite a gate on the left
admits to a strip of unplanted ground, and here starts
a path to Red Pike and the High Stile ridge, which
can be continued to High Crag, Scarth Gap and
Haystacks, joining the valley route at the
Brandreth fence four hours later. This is
hard and rough going.
The alternative route is included on the
accompanying map but not described in
the narrative.

The route crosses an unmetalled road
and a footbridge and joins the main
forest road. Ordinary mortals should
ignore the alternative (above) and
keep plodding on along this road.

(map labels): 2000, 1900, 1800, 1700, 1600, 1500, 1400, 1300, 1200, 1100, 1000

High Stile alternative

route for supermen

800, 700, 600, 500

route for nonsupermen

forest road (19)

footbridge

gate   forest road (20)

Low Gillerthwaite   High Gillerthwaite

gate

River Liza

14   17

High Gillerthwaite is a Youth Hostel
Low Gillerthwaite is a Field Centre (Leeds Metropolitan University)

Ennerdale Forest

Where there are now forest roads in Ennerdale there was once a solitary shepherd's track; where there are now conifers and felled areas there used to be fellsides open to the sky, singing birds and grazing sheep: it was Herdwick country, Cumberland at its best. Those old enough to remember the valley as it once was were saddened by the transformation. Lovers of trees paradoxically do not like the hundreds of thousands that buried Ennerdale: deformed, crowded in a battery, denied light and air and natural growth. Trees ought to be objects of admiration, not pity. Trees have life, but thank goodness they have no feelings, else here would be cruelty on a mammoth scale. (Sentiments like these inspired the Wild Ennerdale initiative — see page 12.)

Pillar Rock and the River Liza

Forestry bridge over the River Liza

The River Liza

The power of a mountain torrent in flood is well exemplified by the River Liza, in dry seasons a wide channel of boulders scoured from the rocky fastnesses at the head of Ennerdale and then rounded and bleached by sun and water, but hidden below a tumultuous cataract in time of spate. The Liza rises near Windy Gap on Great Gable but loses its name in the depths of Ennerdale Water, the outflow being the Ehen.

RED PIKE 2479'

BUTTERMERE

Bleaberry Comb

High Stile alternative route

HIGH STILE 2644'

Burtness Comb

HIGH CRAG 2443'

River Liza

forest road

felled

concrete road bridge

Ennerdale Forest

felled

memorial footbridge

Just keep plodding on along the forest road.

looking back to Pillar and Ennerdale from Loft Beck

ENNERDALE FOREST to LOFT BECK

formerly a shepherd's hut......

Black Sail Youth Hostel

Black Sail Hut is the loneliest and most romantic of Youth Hostels, situated in a magnificent surround of mountainous country. Great Gable dominates the head of the valley with Green Gable and Kirk Fell in support; looking back, Pillar is seen soaring above the forest, and High Crag and Haystacks form an impressive wall to the north. Why go to Switzerland?

The Ennerdale Glacier

The glacier tore away from its moorings on Great Gable at the end of the Ice Age and shuffled down to the sea leaving evidence of its slow journey along the valley. The forest hides many traces but plain to see at the open dalehead are stranded boulders, ice-scratched and polished rocks and a wide area of drumlins, the latter, looking like giant anthills, being clearly in retrospective view on the climb up Loft Beck.

HIGH CRAG 2443'

High Stile alternative route

BUTTERMERE

Scarth Gap

Seat

HAYSTACKS 1959'

Innominate Tarn

WARNSCALE

Blackbeck Tarn

forest road

River Liza

Ennerdale Forest

Black Sail Hut (Youth Hostel)

stile

sheepfold

BLACK SAIL PASS (for) MAIDALE HEAD

drumlins

GREAT GABLE

Loft Beck

All things come to an end. Emergence from the forest is like coming out of a dark room into sunlight. Go past the hut but instead of turning down to the river contour the slope for half a mile to Loft Beck, which ascend steeply by a path on the far bank.

above:
The
Buttermere
valley

left:
Honister
Crag

LOFT BECK to HONISTER PASS

Honister

Honister is well known for its pass, its crag and its slate. The road through the stony defile, once a fearful adventure for waggonettes but now a smooth way for cars, is, on the Buttermere side, a desert of boulders, one of the roughest wildernesses in Lakeland. Impending high above the pass is Honister Crag, a near-vertical precipice honeycombed with quarries where, in defiance of gravity, a beautiful slate is won and taken down to the cutting sheds. The landscape here has been savaged both by nature and man. What a contrast to their joint efforts in nearby Borrowdale!

At the top of Loft Beck take a last look back to Ennerdale and then continue up an easier incline, crossing a post-and-wire fence (the Brandreth fence) and contouring along a cairned path to join the Great Gable track coming in from the right; the point of junction is a fine viewing station for the Buttermere valley. The path, much trodden, now leads gently down to the ruined Drum House, where turn right along the old tramway, descending steeply to the road at the top of Honister Pass. Turn right along it, for Borrowdale.

The Drum House was so called because it operated the cable of the tramway to the cutting sheds.

The Brandreth fence is the suggested rendezvous with any very strong and experienced fellwalkers in the party who may have preferred the High Stile alternative. Sit down and wait for them: they won't be here for hours yet. Don't worry about their safety — they'll be quite all right if they have "THE WESTERN FELLS" with them (ADVT.). When they finally appear, notice how much less strong and much more experienced they look.

The re-union

At almost 2000', this is the highest ground yet reached on the walk.

Where the hell have you been?

Seatoller

From Honister Pass to Seatoller use the old toll road, which is now quite unsuitable for wheeled traffic but is a good alternative to the newer motor road for foot-travellers. At Seatoller (accommodation and café) pass between the houses, turning off at a car park (toilets) to an obvious path beyond: this follows a contour along a wooded fellside in lovely surroundings and, accompanied by the River Derwent, reaches Borrowdale Youth Hostel.

Beyond the Youth Hostel cross the Derwent by a bridge to a lane, turning between the buildings on the left to follow a field-path to the attractive village of Rosthwaite.

Borrowdale

The Lake District is the loveliest part of England, and Borrowdale is the fairest of its valleys. Its appeal lies in the rich tangle of tree and rock — the hanging gardens of birch and rowan, the grey cliffs, that bound its green fields; in its odd configuration, narrowing at mid-valley to the width of road and river but widening at its extremities to form a steep-sided basin for Derwent Water at its foot and a flat strath at its head; in its intriguing side-openings and recesses watered by translucent streams, all beautiful; in its sinuous approach to the highest and finest mountains in the country. Not least of its charms are the clusters of white cottages set amongst its emerald pastures, the centuries-old settlements happily little changed. The picture as a whole is entirely delightful: scenically it is informal to the point of untidiness, yet all things blend in perfect harmony. Man and Nature, working together, have made a good job of Borrowdale.

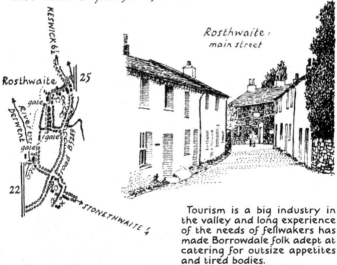

Rosthwaite: main street

Tourism is a big industry in the valley and long experience of the needs of fellwakers has made Borrowdale folk adept at catering for outsize appetites and tired bodies.

Accommodation is provided in every hamlet and at most farmhouses, and in season is in heavy demand; in addition there are camping and caravan sites and two youth hostels. A walker in search of rest and refreshment for the night is advised to start his enquiries at Rosthwaite, the 'capital' of Borrowdale, which has several hotels, a hostel, farmhouse accommodation, a camping barn and a tea room.

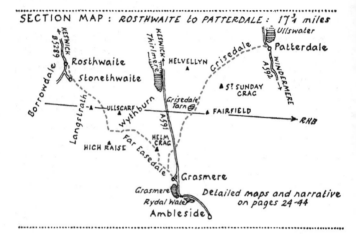

SECTION MAP : ROSTHWAITE to PATTERDALE : 17¼ miles

KESWICK 6835'

Borrowdale

Rosthwaite

Stonethwaite

Langstrath

ULLSCARF

HIGH RAISE

Wythburn

KESWICK Thirlmere

HELVELLYN

A591

Grisedale Tarn

Crisedale

Ullswater

Patterdale

St SUNDAY CRAG

WINDERMERE A592

FAIRFIELD

RHB

Far Easedale

HELM CRAG

Grasmere

Grasmere

Rydal Water

Ambleside

Detailed maps and narrative
on pages 24-44

The route onward from Rosthwaite is barred by a line of
high fells, the first of a succession of long ridges running
north and south across the line of march. These make a
direct beeline for the east impracticable, and the most
pleasurable way of circumventing the series of obstacles
is to take advantage of pedestrian passes through the hills.
Such tactics result in considerable deviations both north
and south of the "straight and narrow" but the zig-zags
recommended will introduce two other places of natural
beauty, Grasmere and Patterdale, while at the same time
making some longitudinal progress east, albeit erratically.
Patterdale is 8 miles due east of Rosthwaite yet the route
described covers twice that distance. But the way is lovely
and the extra miles will not be regretted. A good walker
could reach Patterdale from Rosthwaite comfortably in one
day (turning down Wythburn and crossing Dunmail Raise to
Grisedale Tarn), but it is more rewarding to proceed slowly
in such delectable
surroundings and
devote two days to
the journey with a
stop at Grasmere
overnight.
    The way out of
Rosthwaite starts
along the valley of
Stonethwaite: the
only breach in the
lofty eastern wall
of Borrowdale. It
is a walk in heaven.

Stonethwaite

Borrowdale

WATENDLATH

Rosthwaite

23

29

B 5289

Stonethwaite Beck

Lane

gate

Scafell

road

gate

Stonethwaite

starry saxifrage

Eagle Crag

DOCK TARN

30

400

gate

Galleny Force

gate

300

Langstrath Beck

500

600

700

1200

1000

900

800

600

gap

500

600

Greenup Gill

31

gate

1400

1300

EAGLE CRAG 1650

1600

1500

1400

1300

1600

Long Band

32

Lining Crag

Cross the bridge over Stonethwaite Beck at Rosthwaite, turning right along an old lane and then fields to Stonethwaite Bridge (which do not cross except as a detour to look at the unspoilt and typical hamlet of Stonethwaite). Continue up the valley along a gated bridleway with the beck on the right. In a short mile there is a junction of valleys, Langstrath coming down on the right to a charming meeting of waters. Do not cross the footbridge but keep to the good track climbing steadily alongside Greenup Gill. Look back at Borrowdale before the curve of the valley hides it from sight: a beautiful picture. The impressive Eagle Crag loses its fierce aspect as it is gradually overtopped. Ahead, Lining Crag towers over a prairie of drumlins. Ascend a steep stony gully to the left of it (note the starry saxifrage) and detour to its top, a fine viewpoint, for a well-earned rest.

route

Lining Crag

27

The Wythburn trap

Greenup Edge is a pass between Borrowdale and Grasmere, but do not assume that, once over the summit, the ground in front must immediately descend to Grasmere.   Beyond the pass for a full half mile the descending slopes are those of another valley, Wythburn, into which flow the many streams crossed by the path, and it is a common error, especially in mist, to follow the streams down in the belief that they will lead to Grasmere.   From Greenup Edge there is a glimpse of Grasmere in clear weather and this sets the true direction.

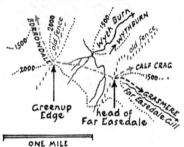

The path, fairly distinct, skirts the headwaters of the Wythburn basin and after an initial descent levels out before slightly rising to another pass, at 1600', which, like Greenup, is crossed by the remains of a wire fence (including a pair of gateposts standing incongruously in isolation).
   This is the true head of Far Easedale, which goes down unerringly, with a good path, to Grasmere.

Let's do a ridge walk

The best form of walking is fell walking and the best part of fell walking is ridge walking and the best part of ridge walking is the traverse of high connecting skylines between neighbouring summits.
   So far in this book the route has preferred lower ground, valleys and passes, in the interests of faster progress, but at the head of Far Easedale there is the opportunity of a simple crossing to a miniature ridge of three summits in direct line for Grasmere, offering a more attractive way thereto than the usual route down the valley.   This ridge walk adds a mile to the journey, requires an extra effort and takes an hour longer — a small price to pay for the advantages of a delectable track, acquaintance with interesting rock formations, and beautiful views.
   So let's do it.

1 : Dollywaggon Pike
2 : St. Sunday Crag
3 : Fairfield
4 : Seat Sandal

looking east from Calf Crag to tomorrow's stage of the walk

The summit rocks,
Calf Crag

Above Lining Crag the slope eases to Greenup Edge, the path being less distinct over peaty ground: follow the cairns (which is not easily done), keeping well to the right. The summit of the pass is marked by an iron stanchion, a relic of a former fence. The mountain panorama here, especially in retrospect, is grand. The path continues clearly down the other side, on rough ground to a lower pass at the head of Far Easedale: on this section do not be deflected into the valley on the left (Wythburn).

At the head of Far Easedale there is a choice of routes:

1: If the weather is fine and time is not pressing, turn left by the old fence and follow a thin undulating track over Calf Crag and beyond down its declining east ridge to Gibson Knott.

2: If the weather is poor, or time is short, or you've had enough climbing for today, or you want to see bog asphodel (a poor excuse) descend into Far Easedale on a path that soon becomes distinct, leading direct, without navigational problems, to Grasmere in 3½ miles.

Helm Crag

better known as 'The Lion and the Lamb'

from Gibson Knott

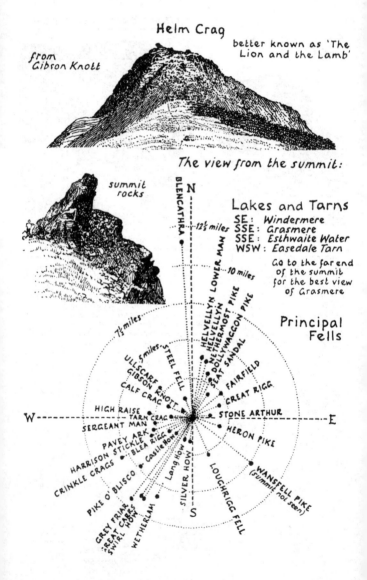

The view from the summit:

summit rocks

Lakes and Tarns

SE: Windermere
SSE: Grasmere
SSE: Esthwaite Water
WSW: Easedale Tarn

Go to the far end of the summit for the best view of Grasmere

Principal Fells

BLENCATHRA
12½ miles
HELVELLYN LOWER MAN
10 miles
HELVELLYN
NETHERMOST PIKE
SEAT SANDAL
DOLLYWAGGON PIKE
FAIRFIELD
GREAT RIGG
STONE ARTHUR
HERON PIKE

7½ miles
5 miles
STEEL FELL
ULLSCARF
GIBSON KNOTT
CALF CRAG

HIGH RAISE
TARN CRAG
SERGEANT MAN
PAVEY ARK
HARRISON STICKLE
CRINKLE CRAGS
BLEA RIGG
Castle How
PIKE O' BLISCO
Long How
GREY FRIAR
GREAT CARRS
SWIRL HOW
WETHERLAM
SILVER HOW
LOUGHRIGG FELL
WANSFELL PIKE
(summit not seen)

W
E
N
S

Grasmere

Grasmere is a lovely village in a setting endowed with sylvan grace and dignity, beloved of artists and poets, and, because of associations with Wordsworth, is known internationally and has become a place of pilgrimage.
It is an excellent overnight halting stage, with much to see and a wide choice of accommodation for both primitive and sophisticated walkers.

Gibson Knott is a switchback ridge with a delightful path that, after a mile of up and down and in and out, crosses a grassy depression and climbs up to the rocky top of Helm Crag (a fascinating place), traverses the summit and descends by a new path (better than the old one) into Easedale, where the direct route is joined. A tarmac road now leads to Grasmere.

direct alternative route

bog asphodel here?

footbridge

bog asphodel

Grasmere Church

Grisedale Pass

The pedestrian route from Grasmere to Patterdale, a splendid walk, lies over the wellknown Grisedale Pass (more correctly but less often named Grisedale Hause), a high corridor reaching 1929 feet between very imposing mountains, typically Lakeland in its atmosphere and character: romantically beautiful at start and finish but sombre and austere in the lofty middle section. A notable feature is Grisedale Tarn at 1768 feet, a large sheet of water in a bowl formed by bare hills; and a most striking and impressive picture is displayed soon afterwards by the wild and craggy eastern coves of the Helvellyn range overlooking the fine valley of Grisedale, the descent into which is a remarkable transition from savage desolation to pastoral loveliness.   The path, also used in the ascent of Helvellyn, is welltrodden and distinct throughout.

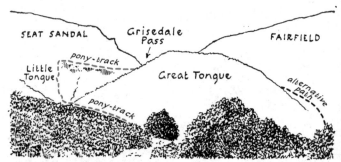

The point of departure from the Grasmere valley is a mile north of the village at Mill Bridge on the main road (A591) to Keswick and is best reached by a quiet byroad turning off the Easedale road at Goody Bridge: this has a fine view up Tongue Gill to Grisedale Pass. At Mill Bridge go up a lane which is signposted 'Public Bridleway Patterdale', climbing by the wooded beck to a confluence of streams at the bottom of Great Tongue. Either side of Great Tongue may be taken: it is usual to bear left on a pony-track and climb Little Tongue (a tedious ascent on grass) for the sake of the retrospective views of Grasmere; at 1600' the track turns to the right above a fringe of rocks and becomes undulating before rising amid stones to the top of Grisedale Pass. (The alternative path east of Great Tongue, starting at a footbridge, is easier; it finally joins the pony-track beyond a series of cascades. The summit of the pass is crossed by an old wall and here there is a view forward of Grisedale Tarn backed by Dollywaggon Pike with a zig-zag scar indicating the Helvellyn path.   Descend to the outlet of the tarn and make a decision (see page 34).

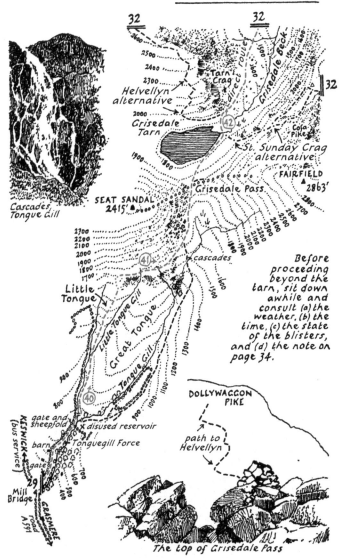

32
32
32

2600
2500
2400
2300
2200

Tarn
Crag

direct route

Grisedale Beck

Helvellyn
alternative

2000

Grisedale Tarn

42

Cofa
Pike

St. Sunday Crag
alternative

1900

1800

FAIRFIELD
▲ 2863'

Grisedale Pass

SEAT SANDAL
2415' ▲

2300
2200
2100
2000
1900
1800
1700

41

cascades

Before
proceeding
beyond the
tarn, sit down
awhile and
consult (a) the
weather, (b) the
time, (c) the state
of the blisters,
and (d) the note on
page 34.

Little
Tongue

Little Tongue Gill

Great Tongue

Tongue Gill

1600
1500
1400
1300
1200

40

900
800

DOLLYWAGGON
PIKE

path to
Helvellyn

KESWICK
(bus service)

gate and
sheepfold

disused reservoir

barn   Tonguegill Force

gate

29

Mill
Bridge

GRASMERE
road A591

700
600
500
400

Cascades,
Tongue Gill

The top of Grisedale Pass

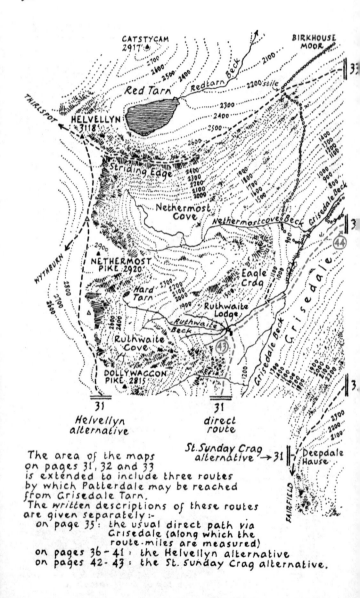

CATSTYCAM
2917'

BIRKHOUSE
MOOR

Red Tarn

Redtarn Beck

2200 stile

HELVELLYN
3118

THIRLSPOT

Striding Edge

Nethermost
Cove

Nethermostcove Beck

Grisedale Beck

WYTHBURN

NETHERMOST
PIKE 2920'

Eagle
Crag

Hard
Tarn

Ruthwaite
Lodge

44

Ruthwaite
Beck

43

Ruthwaite
Cove

Grisedale

Grisedale Beck

DOLLYWAGGON
PIKE 2815'

31

31

Helvellyn
alternative

direct
route

St. Sunday Crag
alternative → 31

Deepdale
Hause

FAIRFIELD

The area of the maps
on pages 31, 32 and 33
is extended to include three routes
by which Patterdale may be reached
from Grisedale Tarn.
The written descriptions of these routes
are given separately :—
  on page 35 : the usual direct path via
                Grisedale (along which the
                route-miles are measured)
  on pages 36-41 : the Helvellyn alternative
  on pages 42-43 : the St. Sunday Crag alternative.

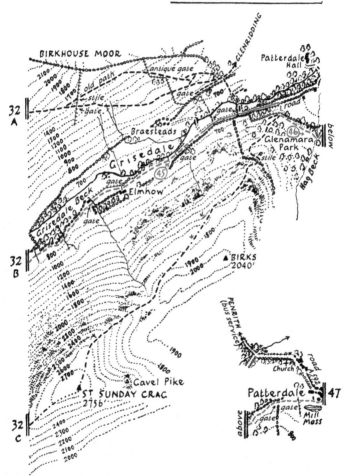

A : The Helvellyn alternative
B : The direct route
C : The St. Sunday Crag alternative

The 'St.' in the name 'St. Sunday Crag' is an abbreviation for 'Saint' (as in St. Bees), not 'Street.'

Let's climb a mountain

The outlet of Grisedale Tarn is a splendid springboard for climbing a mountain on the way to Patterdale (in preference to the direct route, which here commences the long descent into Grisedale), and, if Grasmere was left after breakfast, there should be ample time in hand to do this. The tarn is at 1800', nearly, so that at this point a considerable elevation has already been reached and if the day be fine and settled it seems a pity not to use the height gained to make the ascent of one of the surrounding mountains before taking leave of the Lake District (tomorrow). Lakeland means, to most visitors, not lakes but mountains, and it is fitting that a walk across the district should include a high summit.

Okay then, which one? Well, the two most convenient are HELVELLYN and ST. SUNDAY CRAG, each having a ridge descending to Patterdale. The choice lies between them.

The ascent of Helvellyn (3118') would add two miles and 1500' of climbing to the walk and take two hours longer than the direct route. It has two big attractions apart from its lovely name and literary associations — a very extensive view and the exciting traverse of Striding Edge — but it is a tourists' mountain, very much so: in fact, the most often climbed mountain in the country. The paths, worn as wide as roads, are stony and dusty and noisy with pilgrims.

St. Sunday Crag (2756') is, in sharp contrast, a mountain for connoisseurs: lovely to walk upon, unspoiled, quiet and free from crowds and their attendant litter. It has a classic view of Ullswater. Its ascent would add 1000' of climbing and take an extra hour compared with the way down the valley but in distance is no further.

Walkers who have not yet climbed Helvellyn (if any such there be) will probably prefer to do this. Walkers who have are recommended to try St. Sunday Crag. Neither ascent calls for superhuman ability.

If the rain is pouring down, contemplate neither but go down into Grisedale by the usual direct route.

St. Sunday Crag, from the outlet of Grisedale Tarn

looking down Grisedale
from Ruthwaite

Grisedale Tarn to Patterdale
— the direct route

The direct path to Patterdale along Grisedale is distinct on the ground and calls for little description to supplement the map but certain interesting features are worth mention. Ford the stream issuing from Grisedale Tarn and follow the path ahead, bearing right. Note an outcrop surmounted by a metal sign 60 yards away on the right — this is the Brothers Parting, the place where Wordsworth said a last farewell to his brother John: his verses are inscribed on the rockface. A mile further, the path reaches Ruthwaite Lodge, built in 1854 by the then owner of Patterdale Hall as a rest-house for passing travellers and now occupied by the Ullswater Outward Bound Mountain School. Behind the Lodge are pleasant cascades and old mine levels. The path now descends more sharply by the side of Ruthwaite Beck to a footbridge over Grisedale Beck. In scenery that grows more beautiful every step of the way along the valley, the path continues clearly below the steep slopes of St. Sunday Crag and Birks, becoming a cart-track near the farm at Elmhow and a tarmac road half-a-mile further. A green wrought-iron seat indicates the point where the Helvellyn path joins, and 350 yards further, beyond a plantation, a gate on the right gives access to a pleasant path through Glenamara Park to Patterdale Post Office.

Brothers
Parting

Ruthwaite Lodge

Grisedale Tarn to Patterdale
— the Helvellyn alternative

Gird up your loins, ford the stream issuing from the tarn and bear left to the distinct path climbing up the steep slope in front in a series of zigzags. The gradient eases after an eternity of toil and the path forges ahead rounding the summits of Dollywaggon Pike and Nethermost Pike and finally rising to the top of Helvellyn. In spite of its stones and litter and crowds this is a fine high-level traverse, improved by detours to the right to look down in the vast hollows on the eastern side of the range. If the visibility on Helvellyn is good the panorama pictured on pages 38 to 41 can be checked for accuracy, after which, carefully stepping over the recumbent bodies of exhausted tourists, follow the rim of the summit southeast to Gough's monument, there descending the loose and stony declivity to Striding Edge — an unpleasant descent. The preliminary scramble up onto the Edge may be avoided by a path on the right. Thereafter an easy path runs along it slightly below the crest on the Red Tarn side: this is an exhilarating traverse (the best quarter-mile between St. Bees and Robin Hood's Bay) and it should be lingered over, with frequent moves onto the actual rock crest to savour the airiness of the situation and look for Dixon's Monument. Beyond the dark tower at the end of the Edge life becomes ordinary again and the path gently runs along a declining ridge, passes through the Gap in the Wall (which acquired its name before the gap was filled with a stile) and slants down the flank of Birkhouse Moor to cross a bridge over Grisedale Beck in the valley and so join a tarmac road. Turn left along it and 350 yards further, beyond a plantation, a gate on the right gives access to a pleasant path through Glenamara Park to Patterdale Post Office.

The Monuments of Helvellyn —

The Gough Memorial

Erected 1890 on the rim of the summit above the path to Striding Edge.

This small stone tablet 40 yards south of the shelter commemorates the landing here of an aeroplane in 1926 — a memorable event!

The Dixon Memorial 1858

Situated on a platform of rock on Striding Edge overlooking Nethermost Cove and Grisedale.

Striding Edge

The view from Helvellyn

The figures following the names of fells
indicate distances in miles

N   NE

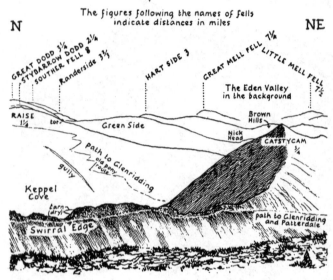

GREAT DODD 3¼ STYBARROW DODD 2¼ SOUTHER FELL 8 Randerside 3⅔ HART SIDE 3 GREAT MELL FELL 7⅛ LITTLE MELL FELL 7½

The Eden Valley
in the background

RAISE 1¼   tor?   Green Side   Brown Hills   Nick Head   CATSTYCAM ¼

Path to Glenridding
old pony route

gully

Keppel
Cove

Tarn (dry)

Swirral Edge

path to Glenridding
and Patterdale

E   SE

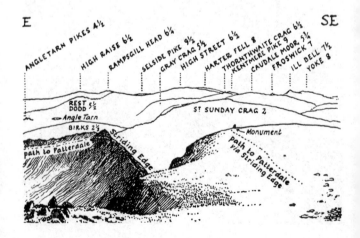

ANGLETARN PIKES 4½ HIGH RAISE 6½ RAMPSGILL HEAD 6¼ SELSIDE PIKE 9½ GRAY CRAG 5½ HIGH STREET 6½ HARTER FELL 8 THORNTHWAITE CRAG 6½ KENTMERE PIKE 9 CAUDALE MOOR 5¾ FROSWICK 7 ILL BELL 7½ YOKE 8

REST DODD 5½   ST SUNDAY CRAG 2

Angle Tarn

BIRKS 2½   Striding Edge   Monument

path to Patterdale   Path to Patterdale
via Striding Edge

The view from Helvellyn

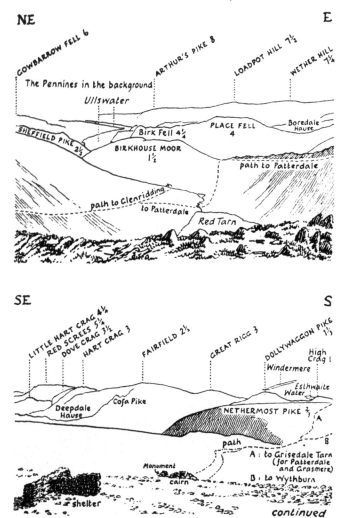

NE

COWBARROW FELL 6

The Pennines in the background

Ullswater

ARTHUR'S PIKE 8

E

LOADPOT HILL 7½

WETHER HILL 7¼

SHEFFIELD PIKE 2½

Birk Fell 4¼

BIRKHOUSE MOOR 1½

PLACE FELL 4

Boredale Hause

path to Patterdale

path to Glenridding

to Patterdale

Red Tarn

SE

LITTLE HART CRAG 4½

RED SCREES 5¼

DOVE CRAG 3½

HART CRAG 3

FAIRFIELD 2½

GREAT RIGG 3

DOLLYWAGGON PIKE 1⅓

S

High Crag 1

Windermere

Esthwaite Water

Deepdale Hause

Cofa Pike

NETHERMOST PIKE ⅔

A

B

path

Monument

cairn

A : to Grisedale Tarn (for Patterdale and Grasmere)

B : to Wythburn

shelter

continued

The view from Helvellyn

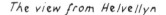

continued

S   **SW**

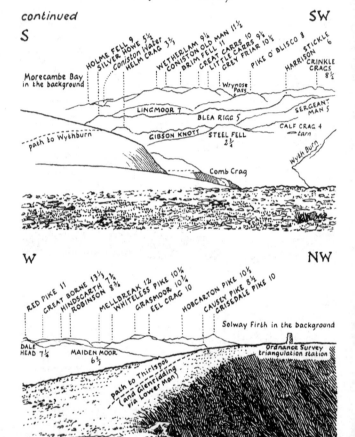

HOLME FELL 9
SILVER HOWE 5½
Coniston Water 3⅔
HELM CRAG 3⅔

WETHERLAM 9¼
CONISTON OLD MAN 11½
BRIM FELL 11
GREAT CARRS 10
LITTLE CARRS 9½
GREY FRIAR 10½

PIKE O' BLISCO 8
HARRISON
STICKLE 6
CRINKLE CRAGS 8½

Morecambe Bay
in the background

Wrynose Pass

LINGMOOR 7

BLEA RIGG 5

SERGEANT MAN 5

path to Wythburn

GIBSON KNOTT

STEEL FELL 2¼

CALF CRAG 4
tarn

Wyth Burn

Comb Crag

W   **NW**

RED PIKE 11
GREAT BORNE 13½
HINDSCARTH 7½
ROBINSON 8½

MELLBREAK 12
WHITELESS PIKE 10½
GRASMOOR 10¾
EEL CRAG 10

HOBCARTON PIKE 10½
CAUSEY PIKE 8½
GRISEDALE PIKE 10

Solway Firth in the background

DALE HEAD 7¼
MAIDEN MOOR 6⅔

Ordnance Survey
triangulation station

Path to Thirlspot
(and Glenridding
via Lower Man)

The view from Helvellyn

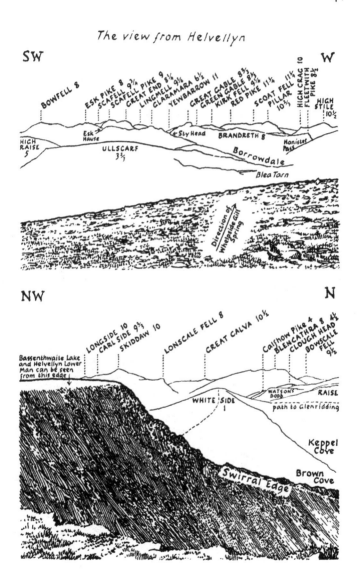

Grisedale Tarn to Patterdale
— the St. Sunday Crag alternative

At the outlet of the tarn turn to the right (east) without crossing the stream. An indistinct path slants upwards over rough slopes, making a beeline for Deepdale Hause (the depression between Fairfield and St. Sunday Crag). After passing a pile of stones turn right up a miniature ridge. If this junction is missed it doesn't matter as the two paths eventually join up just below the hause, where a magnificent view of the cliffs of Fairfield above the wild upper reaches of Deepdale suddenly unfolds, matching in impressiveness the crags and coves of the Helvellyn range across Grisedale. In the midst of profound mountain scenery follow the ridge up to St. Sunday Crag on a distinct path. Near the top the path becomes unclear and disappears. Leave the summit bearing north at first, following a line of cairns, then north-east to an outcropping of rocks (a classic viewpoint), beyond which a rough track descends more steeply to the depression before Birks and slants along its western flank high above Grisedale. The route levels out on a grassy shelf and becomes less clear but cairns lead to a made path descending to a wall (crossed at a stile) enclosing Glenamara Park, through which the path goes down sharp left then right, among trees, to a wire fence. The Grisedale road is now close on the left and can be gained at a gate, but instead turn right, by a wall, on a delightful path that fords Hag Beck and skirts Mill Moss, rampant with rushes and bogbean, just behind Patterdale Post Office.

Ullswater, from the north-east ridge of St. Sunday Crag

The view from St. Sunday Crag

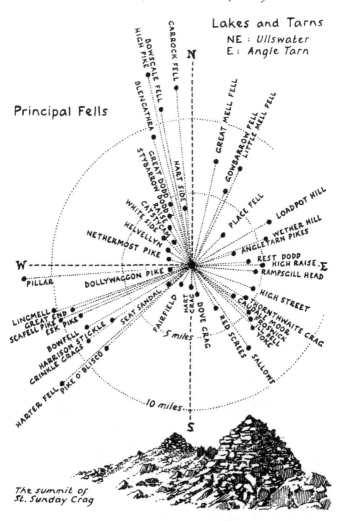

Principal Fells

Lakes and Tarns
NE : Ullswater
E : Angle Tarn

The summit of
St. Sunday Crag

Patterdale

Patterdale is a rival to Borrowdale in the magnificence of its surroundings. Dominated on one side by the rugged mountain wall of the Helvellyn range and on the other by the steep flanks of Place Fell, with, between them, that loveliest of lakes, Ullswater, curving gracefully into the far distance; with crags and heathery fells rising from a strath of emerald valley pastures and a wealth of noble trees, the scene is one of informal but exquisite beauty, and the little village is truly Alpine in situation, aspect and character. Although a place of popular resort and a splendid centre for fellwalkers, Patterdale has not as yet suffered the tourist invasions of Borrowdale and remains unspoilt, presenting a picture that has changed very little during the past century.

The provision of accommodation is a main industry here. Many cottages and farmhouses open their doors to visitors, the village has two hotels and there are more a mile away at Glenridding.   Goldrill Youth Hostel is an excellent building in Scandinavian style, opened 1971.   In summer all this accommodation is heavily in demand and should be reserved in advance.

Before turning in for the night take a stroll across the valley to the lakeside path below Place Fell for a view of Ullswater that is unsurpassed for loveliness.

The head of Ullswater

SECTION MAP : *PATTERDALE to SHAP : 16 miles*

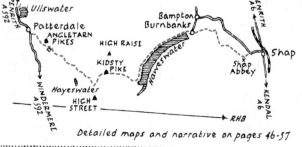

Detailed maps and narrative on pages 46-57

The journey from Patterdale to Shap involves a lofty crossing of the High Street massif, the final mountain barrier of Lakeland in the east, and during the course of the walk the scenery changes dramatically, sombre fells giving place to a pastoral limestone landscape. This is farewell to Lakeland, and farewells to Lakeland are always sad. What follows is anti climax — level walking instead of up and down, trees and fields and villages instead of rough and lonely hills: lovely, yes, but not excitingly beautiful as the crossing of Lakeland has been. Well, it's not too late to abandon the coast to coast idea and stay on in Patterdale. There is nothing ahead as good, admittedly — the big fault of doing this walk in a west to east direction is that the best comes first. Anyway, please yourself. Stay if you want to and I'll carry on alone, and no hard feelings. You'll think of something to tell the folks at home.... Mind, you might find yourself thinking in the next few days about Shap and the limestone plateau beyond, and wondering what Swaledale is really like and whether the North York Moors are as attractive as people say. You *could* have regrets. And (let's be clear about this) you can't expect to get your money back for the book if you prefer not to continue the walk...... Coming with me? Good. I thought you would.

In clear weather the High Street crossing is without difficulties and indeed is a most exhilarating march. If there is rain or mist it is advisable to avoid it (unless the route is remembered from previous visits) and instead use the lakeside path to Howtown followed by a road almost to Pooley Bridge and a path across Moor Divock to Helton, then a quiet road through Bampton to Shap (all clearly shown on the Ordnance Survey map): a long but easy walk (19 miles) that could be shortened by four miles (as can the High Street route) by making Bampton the overnight objective.

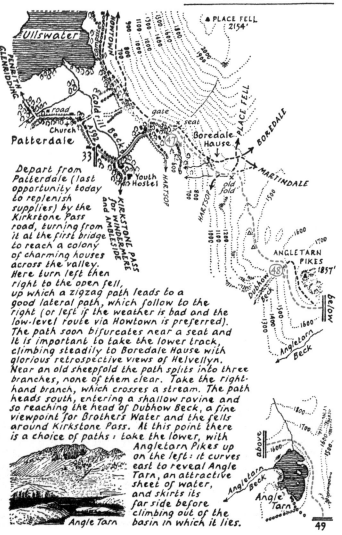

Angle Tarn

Depart from Patterdale (last opportunity today to replenish supplies) by the Kirkstone Pass road, turning from it at the first bridge to reach a colony of charming houses across the valley. Here turn left then right to the open fell, up which a zigzag path leads to a good lateral path, which follow to the right (or left if the weather is bad and the low-level route via Howtown is preferred). The path soon bifurcates near a seat and it is important to take the lower track, climbing steadily to Boredale Hause with glorious retrospective views of Helvellyn. Near an old sheepfold the path splits into three branches, none of them clear. Take the right-hand branch, which crosses a stream. The path heads south, entering a shallow ravine and so reaching the head of Dubhow Beck, a fine viewpoint for Brothers Water and the fells around Kirkstone Pass. At this point there is a choice of paths: take the lower, with Angletarn Pikes up on the left: it curves east to reveal Angle Tarn, an attractive sheet of water, and skirts its far side before climbing out of the basin in which it lies.

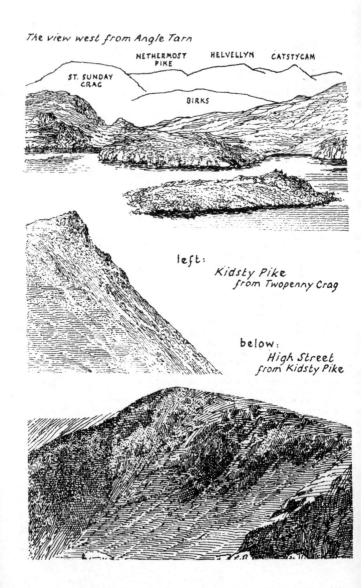

The view west from Angle Tarn

ST. SUNDAY CRAG — NETHERMOST PIKE — HELVELLYN — CATSTYCAM — BIRKS

left:
Kidsty Pike
from Twopenny Crag

below:
High Street
from Kidsty Pike

47

49 ← The 49th mile appears on the 49th page. By a rapid calculation it will be ascertained that we are so far averaging a mile a page.

▲ REST DODD 2283

gap Satura Crag

The valley descending north from Satura Crag is Bannerdale. The valley descending north of The Knott is Rampsgill. They join in Martindale, a deer preserve.

The deeply inurned tarn down on this side is Hayeswater (a reservoir). The cluster of buildings lower down its valley is the hamlet of Hartsop.

RAMPSGILL HEAD 2598 ▲

HIGH RAISE

THE KNOTT 2423

HARTSOP

KIDSTY PIKE 2560

Twopenny Crag

Straits of Riggindale

Riggindale

51

ROMAN ROAD

With Angle Tarn left behind and out of sight the path continues over Satura Crag, where care is needed to avoid taking a turning on the left. Then the path descends a little to cross wet peaty ground, the only excitement hereabouts being generated by the reflection that fifty miles of the journey have now been accomplished. Already it seems ages since Cleator and Nannycatch! Now follows a tedious climb around the shoulder of The Knott, passing a turning on the right that leads downhill to Hayeswater and Hartsop, and anyone who is regretting having left Patterdale and wishing to return to it for an extended stay (and be damned to the Coast to Coast Walk) may use this pleasant alternative route to do so.

HIGH STREET 2718
Ordnance Survey column

Others, more resolute, will toil onwards and reap their reward when, beyond The Knott, they reach a point on the main ridge overlooking a depression (the Straits of Riggindale) and find themselves suddenly looking down Riggindale to Haweswater and Mardale Head, with Kidsty Pike and High Street framing the picture. High Street is massively attractive, its Roman road showing clearly, and its summit is easily reached from here but if the hour is already past noon there really isn't time to do it. Instead, take the path branching over Twopenny Crag (named pre-decimalisation) and skirting the rim of Riggindale — very easy walking — to Kidsty Pike: its summit is the best station for taking a last long look at the serrated mountain skyline of Lakeland, the like of which will not be seen again this side of the North Sea. But there will be other years, other visits..... The hills will wait.

50

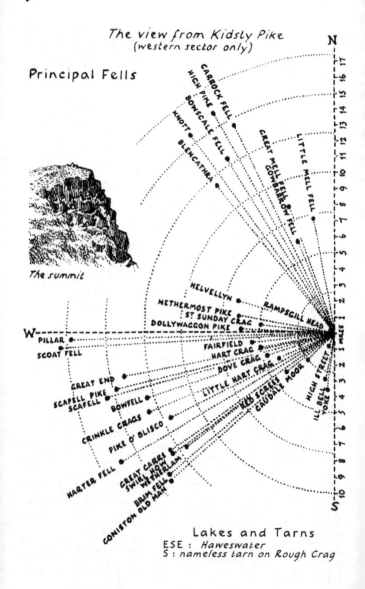

The view from Kidsty Pike
(western sector only)

Principal Fells

Lakes and Tarns
ESE : *Haweswater*
S : *nameless tarn on Rough Crag*

KIDSTY PIKE to WHELTER KNOTTS

The descent from Kidsty Pike is simple. A thin cairned track goes easily down the east ridge and continues to Kidsty Howes, an interesting area of rocky hillocks. The path from here to the stone bridge over Randale Beck has appeared since the Coast to Coast Walk was devised. In this area are the sad remains of Riggindale Farm, a victim of the transformation of Haweswater into a reservoir. Note the newly-planted trees at the head of the lake.

At the stone bridge the fellside path engineered by Manchester Corporation is reached. Followed to the right it leads to the road-end at Mardale Head in a mile (no accommodation now). Our way is to the left, and although the path is overgrown with bracken in places (especially below Whelter Knotts, where Manchester should send a man with a scythe annually in August) there is no danger of straying from it — it accompanies a wall or fence throughout the full length of the lake (sorry, reservoir) and is nowhere more than 30 yards from it. The only points of interest are Birks Crag, the top of which is the site of a British fort, and the crossing of Whelter Beck — note the waterfall under the bridge.

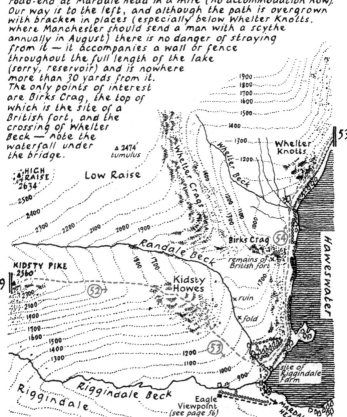

↑ This is what happens when a lake is converted to a reservoir ↓

Mardale

Only people who are now over eighty will remember Mardale as a charming and secluded valley — before its lake was 'promoted' to reservoir, and can bring to mind the natural beaches, where primroses fringed the banks, that are now sterile shores, arid and lifeless, sometimes beneath the water, sometimes not; or the farms and drystone walls that were engulfed and today are revealed as skeletons in times of drought; or the lane that returns to daylight, now recognisable only by tumbled hedgerows, at periods of low water. They mourn its passing, for Mardale then was lovely.

ONE INCH = TWO MILES

Shading indicates the natural Haweswater, the black line the artificial shore of the reservoir.

Church Inn } Mardale Green

HAWESWATER BEFORE AND AFTER

Haweswater from Measand

This section calls for little comment. The way is obvious and straightforward and the path, now improving, is pleasant for both feet and eyes although views of Haweswater along here are obscured by trees. The best natural feature is Measand Forces, a spectacular tangle of rocks and waterfalls, known sufficiently to attract a few visitors on most summer days, the popular approach being from Burnbanks. The path now assumes the width of a cart-track. An item of interest, seen before reaching the Haweswater dam, is the entrance to the reservoir of the tunnelled Heltondale supply, while opposite across the water is glimpsed the outflow of the tunnel from Swindale.

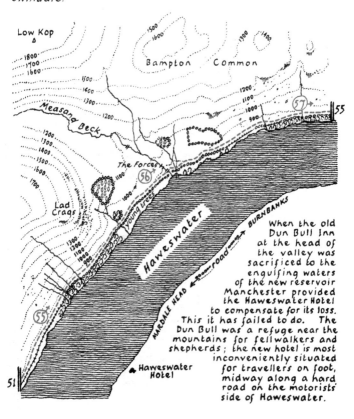

Low Kop

Bampton Common

Measand Beck

The Forces

Lad Crags

Haweswater

MARDALE HEAD ← road → BURNBANKS

Young Trees

Haweswater Hotel

When the old Dun Bull Inn at the head of the valley was sacrificed to the engulfing waters of the new reservoir Manchester provided the Haweswater Hotel to compensate for its loss. This it has failed to do. The Dun Bull was a refuge near the mountains for fellwalkers and shepherds; the new hotel is most inconveniently situated for travellers on foot, midway along a hard road on the motorists' side of Haweswater.

It is a fact that route-finding in cultivated valleys and in low pastures is more prone to error than on desolate mountains. In this section the route follows footpaths (shown on the Ordnance maps) that have obviously fallen into disuse and can no longer be discerned on the ground, but the scenery is ample compensation. Refer to the facing map and following notes as doubts arise.

Burnbanks is reached from a gate in the plantation fence, a road winding down through new houses on the site of the bungalows of the reservoir employees, set pleasantly among trees. At the junction by the telephone box go straight on along an attractive path through woodland. When you come to a road take the stile opposite, passing a notice board giving details of the natural history of the area. The path crosses Haweswater Beck and Naddle Beck in quick succession. After a wall is crossed there is a view on the left of Thornthwaite Force, which is best seen in winter, when the trees are bare. Follow the beck downstream to Park Bridge and continue along the cart track ahead. This aims for Low Park, but after the second gate go up the field sharp right to High Park, continuing in the same direction, on an invisible footpath, to Rawhead and the Swindale road.

Cross the open common ahead, inclining left to Rosgill Bridge (Shap can be reached by road from here, saving half an hour). Without crossing the bridge, go through a gate on the right and along a green road running parallel with the river. After a second gate bear left, following first a wall and then a fence to a charming packhorse bridge, which, having regard to the obvious non-use of the paths to and from it, is seldom visited. Across it, go up to a ruined farm building beyond which is a road. Keep on this road, up the hill, and turn left at a stile where the wall becomes close to the road. After crossing another stile continue in the same direction, passing a wall corner on the right and crossing a large field to a stile in the far corner with the wooded valley of the River Lowther near ahead. Turn right in the next field to a stile in the wall above Abbey Bridge. The Abbey is in full view and can be visited. A concrete road winds uphill beyond the bridge, but the route goes across a field, uphill, to cut the corner off. Soon be there now...

Packhorse bridge,
Swindale Beck

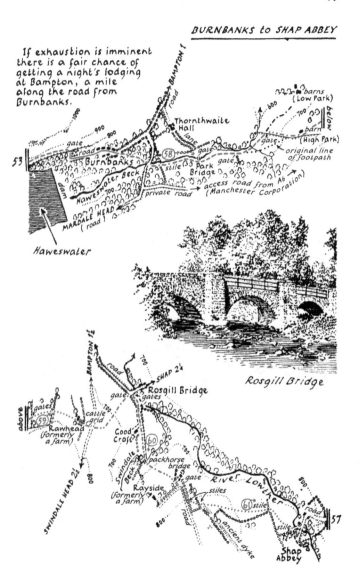

If exhaustion is imminent there is a fair chance of getting a night's lodging at Bampton, a mile along the road from Burnbanks.

BAMPTON 1

road

Thornthwaite Hall

lane

Burnbanks

Haweswater Beck

MARDALE HEAD (road)

Haweswater

dam

stile

Park Bridge

private road

access road from Ab (Manchester Corporation)

barns (Low Park)

barn (High Park)

original line of footpath

below

gate

Rosgill Bridge

BAMPTON 1½

road

SHAP 2¼

Rosgill Bridge

gates

gate

above

gate

cattle grid

Rawhead (formerly a farm)

Good Croft

Swindale Beck

packhorse bridge

Rayside (formerly a farm)

road

gate

stiles

River Lowther

ancient dyke

stile

road

Shap Abbey

SWINDALE HEAD 2¼

Shap Abbey

The builders of England's ancient country abbeys were not only experts in a craft now either extinct or dormant but landscape artists too: they certainly had a good eye for the most-favoured and pleasantest rural locations. Quiet retreats in sequestered valleys, amidst trees and with a river nearby: these were the requisites and it is small wonder that, in such peaceful surroundings, the buildings too had grace and dignity and beauty.

Shap Abbey, built in the 12th and 13th centuries, conforms to this pattern. It stands deep in the wooded valley of the River Lowther, so that it is not seen until the last moments of approach, when the tower reveals its fine proportions. Little else remains above first-floor height and much has been lost, but the arrangement of the various buildings is clear on the ground.

The ruins are in the good care of English Heritage, and admission is free. Near by is a painting of the abbey as it was before it became a ruin.

Shap Abbey
from the north

Incidentally (although this has nothing to do with Shap Abbey) that large bird you saw as you came over the mountains from Patterdale might well have been a golden eagle, as you thought. In 1969 eagles returned to nest in the Lake District after an absence of more than a century and successfully reared young, but since 2004 there has only been a solitary male in residence. The eyries are located in the crags to the south of Riggindale in sight of the east ridge of Kidsty Pike. Viewing facilities are provided by the Royal Society for the Protection of Birds.

The road, enclosed by walls that provide evidence of our arrival in limestone terrain, leads directly to the north end of Shap village, but can be avoided by a path on its north side which visits a rounded grassy hump

that indicates a tumulus. Rejoin the road at a gate and proceed to the once-busy A6. Turn to the right to seek a bed and food.

17th Century Market Hall, Shap

Shap

Shap has been a by-word amongst road travellers since stage-coach days. For many the very name invokes vivid memories of hazardous journeys in snow and storm and mist over the A6, the highest main road in the country, nearly 1400' at its summit in a wilderness of moors. The A6 is a road with a notorious history of accidents but its importance as a main traffic artery to Scotland, however, was greatly diminished at a stroke by the opening on a day in October 1970 of the motorway M6, this taking an easier, lower and less exposed route through the hills. This was a red letter day for some Shap folk, a black letter day for others. The A6 suddenly became quiet. Commerce suffered but, overnight, Shap became a better place to live.

The village straddles the A6 a few miles to the north of its summit: a mile-long village with little breadth, clinging to the road as to a lifeline. It has a few pleasant nooks and corners but is generally unattractive. Its economy is based on the road and railway and especially on the huge granite works and limestone quarries, none of them the source of any beauty or relieving the bleak landscape.

Many hotels and boarding-houses and cafés line the A6, more perhaps than are now required. Shap will live on, but its name will mean nothing to future generations of tourists and lorry-drivers.

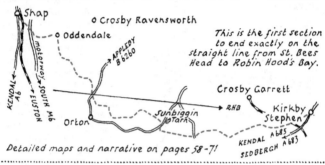

SECTION MAP : *SHAP to KIRKBY STEPHEN*: 20 miles

This is the first section to end exactly on the straight line from St. Bees Head to Robin Hood's Bay.

Detailed maps and narrative on pages 58-71.

The terrain between Shap and Kirkby Stephen takes the form of a limestone plateau, elevated at about the 1000' contour, and, as every walker knows, a limestone footing invariably means easy travelling on velvet turf, especially when the rock is outcropping or just below the surface, while its appearance when exposed to weather —crinkled, fissured and often grotesquely sculptured— allied to its glittering whiteness in sunlight, is a delight to the eye always. Mountain limestone is, of course, the great favourite as the basis of rock gardens, and a few areas have been denuded of surface stone by exploiters of this demand, but their activities are now, properly, subject to strict planning control. Many of the escarpments and creviced 'pavements' met on the walk are very fine, but the waterworn caves and potholes peculiar to limestone formations are singularly absent in this district.

This section of the walk is also out of the ordinary by reason of its prolific evidences of prehistoric and primitive settlements : hut-villages, stone circles and tumuli are all present in the vicinity, indicating that large communities existed here before the dawn of history, scraping a poor livelihood from land that remains today inhospitable, bare and uncultivated.   The ancient settlements near Crosby Ravensworth and Crosby Garrett in particular are of outstanding interest and represent Westmorland's main contribution to archaeological research. Some of these relics of the past will be visited along the route.

The flora of limestone country, too, is a constant joy, the deep crevices harbouring flowers and ferns and mosses in variety; indeed, most limestone outcroppings are complete natural rock gardens furnished with shy and delicate plants, some such as the bird's eye primrose, rare elsewhere, being commonplace locally.

Primula farinosa

A walker on limestone is well favoured.

Paths east of Shap have been disturbed by the motorway, but footbridges have been provided at two points. The village is now most conveniently left by a street directly opposite the Kings Arms Hotel on the A6, leading to a housing estate. Here turn right into a lane bending left to a bridge over the railway, beyond which it runs between walls under an electricity cable. At a fork bear right and cross three fields (the indistinct path is indicated by stiles) to reach a conspicuous footbridge crossing the motorway: an expensive structure for a path so little used. Over the footbridge keep alongside the fence to the right. At a copse of hawthorns a thin track will be found inclining left uphill—note the many granite boulders scattered around— to a gate near a farmhouse (Nab House), through which the road to Hardendale is crossed, the route continuing over a pleasant pasture on the same contour with a limestone scar on the left. When a wall is reached follow it up to the left to a stile in a vanished fence. Ahead the scene is downright ugly, an active limestone quarry causing widespread devastation. A stile on the right leads to a place where the rights of walkers are preserved (the former footpath having been blasted out of existence) by two flights of wood steps where the access road runs in a cutting. Across this road keep on in the same direction, soon joining an unmetalled road heading straight for Oddendale, the cluster of buildings in this farming hamlet being hidden by trees. The map below shows how the area covered by the quarry has increased since 1972. The new workings are largely hidden from view by an embankment.

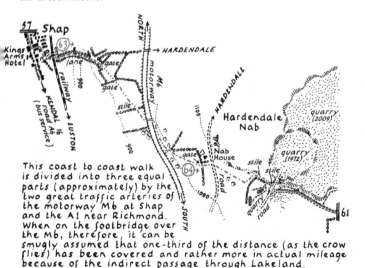

This coast to coast walk is divided into three equal parts (approximately) by the two great traffic arteries of the motorway M6 at Shap and the A1 near Richmond. When on the footbridge over the M6, therefore, it can be smugly assumed that one-third of the distance (as the crow flies) has been covered and rather more in actual mileage because of the indirect passage through Lakeland.

Antiquities of Crosby Ravensworth Fell

HIGH STREET   KIDSTY PIKE   HIGH RAISE

Stone Circle near Oddendale, looking west to Lakeland

Robin Hood's Grave

Erratic boulders:
Granite resting on
limestone

Monument, Black Dub

This bears the following
inscription:

HERE AT BLACK DUB
THE SOURCE OF THE LIVENNET
KING CHARLES THE II
REGALED HIS ARMY
AND DRANK OF THE WATER
ON HIS MARCH FROM SCOTLAND
AUGUST 8 1651

ODDENDALE to ROBIN HOOD'S GRAVE

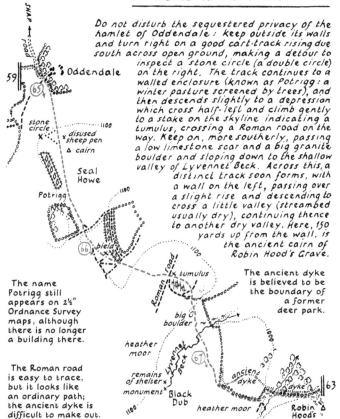

Do not disturb the sequestered privacy of the hamlet of Oddendale: keep outside its walls and turn right on a good cart-track rising due south across open ground, making a detour to inspect a stone circle (a double circle) on the right. The track continues to a walled enclosure (known as Potrigg: a winter pasture screened by trees), and then descends slightly to a depression which cross half-left and climb gently to a stake on the skyline indicating a tumulus, crossing a Roman road on the way. Keep on, more southerly, passing a low limestone scar and a big granite boulder and sloping down to the shallow valley of Lyvennet Beck. Across this, a distinct track soon forms, with a wall on the left, passing over a slight rise and descending to cross a little valley (streambed usually dry), continuing thence to another dry valley. Here, 150 yards up from the wall, is the ancient cairn of Robin Hood's Grave.

The ancient dyke is believed to be the boundary of a former deer park.

The name Potrigg still appears on 2½" Ordnance Survey maps, although there is no longer a building there.

The Roman road is easy to trace, but it looks like an ordinary path; the ancient dyke is difficult to make out.

Crosby Ravensworth Fell

Crosby Ravensworth today is the quietest of villages and its serenity is profound, but in primitive times it centred a community of some importance, the surrounding countryside being colonised on a rough social pattern, as is evidenced by the plentiful remains of earthworks. The Romans, too, built their road from Low Borrow Bridge to Brougham through here.

Castle Folds

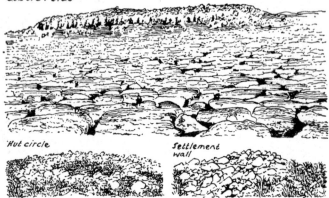

'Hut circle'   Settlement wall

From Robin Hood's Grave return to and accompany the wall until it turns sharp left, when keep on ahead over the brow of the hill and so reach the Crosby Ravensworth road in the vicinity of a disused quarry. Cross over the road and take a faint path heading for the left corner of a wood. The path eventually comes out at the junction of the Appleby and Crosby Ravensworth roads. Here, on the edge of Orton Scar, there is a magnificent view forward of the upper Lune Valley backed by the Howgill Fells.

From here the route originally headed east, passing the monument on Beacon Hill (illustrated on the opposite page) and the ancient settlement of Castle Folds (illustrated above), but the route was diverted at the request of the landowner. Now the original route is entirely within a designated area of public access and could be revived, but there is still a wall to be climbed, and it is better to use the route described here.

Cross the cattle grid and bear left along a grassy track with a wall on the left. At a well-preserved limekiln bear right passing between two walls. Go through the gate ahead, and keep to the left-hand side of the field until you come to the drive of Broadfell Farm. Turn left here, and left again in a quarter of a mile into Street Lane, a traffic-free road with grass growing along its centre in places. As soon as the third farm (Scarside) is passed, go through a gate and follow a fence half-left to a wall. Fifty yards along the wall a stile gives access to Knott Lane. The route continues over the stile directly opposite, but a few yards along the lane to the right there is a view through a gateway on the left of the prehistoric stone circle known as Gamelands or the Druidical Temple. It is made up entirely of erratic boulders brought to this area by glaciers.

Snacks and refreshments are available in the village of Orton which may be reached by the B6260, or by taking the delightful bridleway through Broadfell Farm.

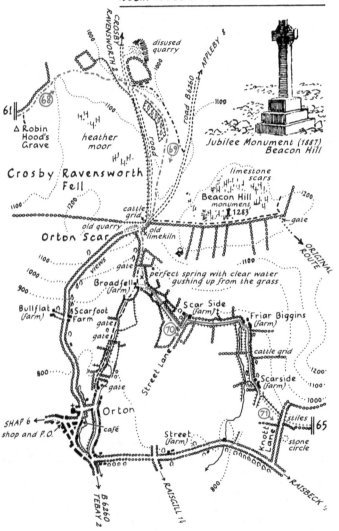

Jubilee Monument (1887)
Beacon Hill

Sunbiggin Tarn, with the major spring in the foreground

Sunbiggin Tarn

Sunbiggin Tarn has many regular visitors, but none of them would describe it as visually attractive: it is little more than a large reedy pond in the middle of a morass. Its attractions lie in other directions, mainly as a haunt and nesting-place of water-fowl in variety— this is a rewarding 'station' for birdwatchers. Botanists too find delight on the limestone banks nearby. It is a suntrap and, thanks (or otherwise) to the public road alongside, a popular picnic-place. The geology is also interesting: note how the limestone below the road ends abruptly along a line where many springs bubble to the surface; the tarn itself, of course, occupies a basin of impermeable rock.

Rayseat Pike Long Barrow

The barrow from the south

The long barrow on Rayseat Pike is one of the best relics of its kind and possibly the earliest evidence of the prehistory of Westmorland. It was excavated, examined and measured in 1875, the search revealing the remains of both adults and children. An unexpected discovery was a cremation trench containing many burnt bones, a feature that has caused speculation as to the age of this ancient burial ground. The dimensions of the barrow were ascertained as 179 feet in length with a width tapering from 62 feet to 36 feet.

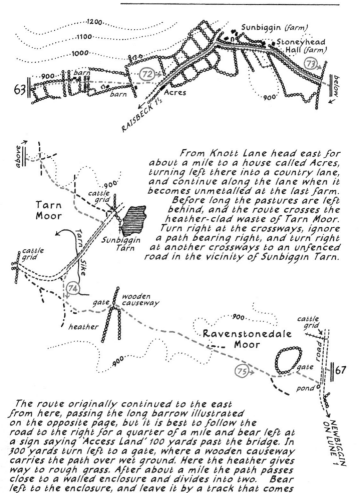

From Knott Lane head east for about a mile to a house called Acres, turning left there into a country lane, and continue along the lane when it becomes unmetalled at the last farm. Before long the pastures are left behind, and the route crosses the heather-clad waste of Tarn Moor. Turn right at the crossways, ignore a path bearing right, and turn right at another crossways to an unfenced road in the vicinity of Sunbiggin Tarn.

The route originally continued to the east from here, passing the long barrow illustrated on the opposite page, but it is best to follow the road to the right for a quarter of a mile and bear left at a sign saying 'Access Land' 100 yards past the bridge. In 300 yards turn left to a gate, where a wooden causeway carries the path over wet ground. Here the heather gives way to rough grass. After about a mile the path passes close to a walled enclosure and divides into two. Bear left to the enclosure, and leave it by a track that comes out on an unfenced road by a pond. Turn left for 100 yards and then right onto an unmetalled road.

Severals Village Settlement

The Royal Commission on Ancient Monuments included in their inventory for Westmorland (1935) references to a complex of prehistoric villages, comprising stone-walled fields, hutments, dykes and pathways, on the south-east slope of the fellside above Smardale, describing this as a key site and one of the most remarkable in Britain.

These enthusiastic references lead a visitor to expect more than there is in fact to be seen, at least by expert eyes: indeed a man with other matters on his mind could walk across the site without noticing any features out of the ordinary, while a man of greater observation may be vaguely puzzled to see the ground apparently divided by low embankments into compartments but probably attach no importance or significance to this fragmentary evidence of past use of the land. To trained eyes, however, there is a story to be learnt from these primitive earthworks: the parapets are the foundations of former walls, marking boundaries and enclosing fields, the sunken ways were farm tracks, the small patterned areas are the traces of stone huts. Men lived here, as a community, where no men now live and few men ever come: the site is very remote and today rarely visited.

It is a place that would be better appreciated from an aerial view than a tour of the ground. The site has never been excavated; if it were to be a gap in our knowledge of the early settlers in the district might well be bridged.

YARDS
0   100   200

stile
Severals
1000
modern stone wall
900   900
Severals
quarry
limestone outcrops
railway cottages (unoccupied)
Severals Gill
low limestone escarpment
tarn
track of former railway
railway bridge
notice board
800
Scandal Beck
Smardale Bridge

There are three villages, contiguous but separated today by the modern stone wall. Our route passes close to the largest of these, now known as Severals Settlement.

RAVENSTONEDALE MOOR to SMARDALE BRIDGE

When the unmetalled road ends at a covered reservoir continue in the same direction. There follows a long mile of fast walking with splendid views of Mallerstang Edge, Wild Boar Fell and the Howgill Fells forward and to the right. Beyond Bents Farm (where there is a camping barn) the ground is much churned up by tractors. A gate in the intake wall gives access to a large pasture. Watch carefully for the stile in the crosswall shown on the map: without its help the wall cannot be negotiated. Now continue along the wall, keeping left of the earthworks of the ancient village settlement.

Use a gate near the tarn at the bottom of the field to cross the old railway track by a bridge and turn to the right to descend to Smardale Bridge in an area of prehistoric remains. Sunlight clearly defines the regular pillow mounds (the so-called Giants' Graves) high on the far slope of the beck.

The defunct railway was a link between main lines at Tebay and Kirkby Stephen. It closed down in 1962. It is now an excellent dry level footpath, part of the Smardale Gill National Nature Reserve run by the Cumbria Wildlife Trust. The reserve is noted for its bird's-eye primroses and butterfly orchids, and it is one of only two places in England where Scotch argus butterflies are found. The path may be joined using the stile at the south end of the footbridge. There are interesting notice boards along the path in both directions.

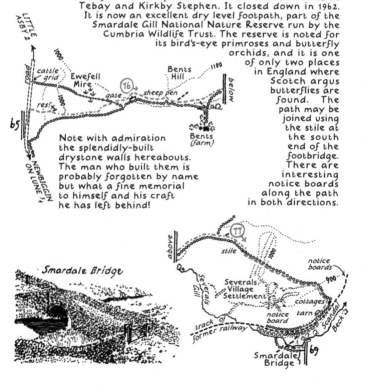

Note with admiration the splendidly-built drystone walls hereabouts. The man who built them is probably forgotten by name but what a fine memorial to himself and his craft he has left behind!

Smardale Bridge

Pillow Mounds, Smardale Bridge

In the vicinity of Smardale Bridge are many raised mounds, rectangular in plan, about 15 yards long and 5 yards wide, and obviously not natural formations. They were formerly indicated on Ordnance maps as 'Giants' Graves' — the name attributed to them by local informants at the time of the first survey — but they are now described as 'Pillow Mounds'.

The purpose of these pillow mounds is still obscure, the only certain thing being that they are not graves of giants. Similar ancient mounds in other parts of the country have been identified as warrens made by man to facilitate the breeding and capture of rabbits, but here, in Smardale, this explanation is unlikely to apply, for their proximity to the village settlements strongly suggests an association. Rabbits were not introduced to this country until after the 11th century but the settlements (and mounds) almost certainly date back to the dawn of history. The mounds have the appearance of long barrows or burial sites — but this possibility is discounted by the best authorities, who seem more prepared to accept the theory, pending verification, that they may well have been constructed as platforms for stacking bracken.

There is a field of enquiry waiting near Smardale Bridge for an archaeologist with a spade.

Smardale
with two pillow mounds in the foreground

SMARDALE BRIDGE to LIMEKILN HILL

Cross Smardale Bridge and continue uphill on a cart-track between walls. From a stile on the left, after 200 yards, there is a good view of Smardale Gill and the railway viaduct. At a bend in the wall beyond a gate in a fence there is a close view, over the wall, of two of the pillow mounds so numerous in this locality. Further, a gate in a crosswall at a sheepfold admits to the large open moorland of Smardale Fell, where a distinct path, used by quad bikes, goes forward over the crest of a minor undulation with a curiously narrow enclosure a mile long on the left and a small conical hill on the right. The walking now is excellent, amongst intermittent heather and limestone outcrops. When the wall trends away left, a branch path follows it down to Smardale Hall: ignore this, and keep on forward over another undulation, now with a fine view ahead across the valley of the River Eden to Nine Standards Rigg, Mallerstang Edge and the long high skyline of the Pennines — the next stage of the journey. A wall is met and accompanied downhill, crossing a muddy patch and passing two old limekilns, the first near-perfect, the second collapsed (even more so than when it was illustrated).

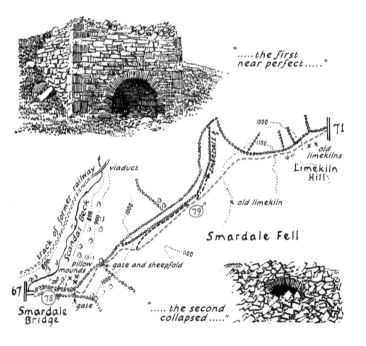

".....the first near perfect....."

1000

71

1100

× old limekilns

Limekiln Hill

SMARDALE

× old limekiln

Smardale Fell

viaduct

79

1000

900

800

1100

700

600

pillow mounds

gate and sheepfold

67

78

1000

gate

Smardale Bridge

track of former railway

Scandal Beck

"..... the second collapsed ....."

Village Settlements, Waitby

After leaving the Waitby road, the route crosses a pasture that has obvious traces of the earthworks of an old settlement, then passes under the railway bridge to another field, where, immediately on the right amongst scattered hawthorns, are the equally distinct evidences of two other settlements, the southern parts of which were destroyed during the construction of the railway except for sections still visible on the other side. All these remains, consisting mainly of raised parapets, are easily traced and reveal irregular enclosures and hut circles.

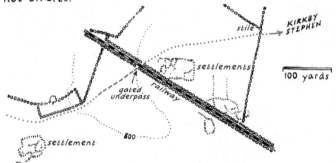

Kirkby Stephen

Kirkby Stephen is an obvious staging-post on the walk, a place for licking wounds and replenishing supplies. Here are shops and cafés galore, many hotels, a youth hostel and much private accommodation. Although but a small town of less than 2000 population it is in fact the largest community so far met on the walk, and in the distance remaining to be travelled only Richmond offers comparable facilities.

It is the market town for a wide rural area and therefore is a busy little place, yet it is away from main tourist routes and remains unspoiled. The A685 running through it carries traffic between the north-east and the Lancashire coast and comes to life when the Blackpool 'lights' are 'on'. There is a variety of religious establishments, the principal being the Parish Church of St Stephen, and this and other buildings in and around the Market Place have interesting features.

The town has length but little width. It hugs the A685 for a mile almost without built-up offshoots. Unseen from the main thoroughfare but confining the town on the east is the River Eden, not far travelled from its source in the hills of Mallerstang but already a considerable watercourse. It goes on to enter the Solway Firth near Carlisle.

At a gate a minor road (to Smardale) is reached. Walk right along the road to a junction where turn left down the Waitby road. Leave this at a 'Coast to Coast' signpost on the right to descend a pasture between a walled enclosure (left) and the earthworks of an ancient settlement (right) to an underpass on the railway ahead (this is the Settle to Carlisle line). Beyond the underpass, in the next field, are traces of more settlements. A stile in the far corner (east) admits to a large pasture crossed by a broken fence. A cream-topped post shows the way. A path is found that passes down a shallow valley, inclining right to a stile in a wall near a clump of larch trees. From this go down a field past a barn to a gate at the bottom. Ahead, two underpasses in quick succession lead beneath the two branches of a disused railway to the environs of Greenriggs Farm, bypassed by two gates on the left (or, more easily, go through the farmyard), so joining a lane that leads in a short mile alongside the flat-topped hill of Croglam Castle (not worth a detour) to Kirkby Stephen. The lane becomes a back street for houses on the main road (the A685), which can be joined at a tarmac link (opposite a recreation ground), emerging 200 yards south of the Youth Hostel. Turn left for the town centre.

The Stainmore Railway Company was formed in 2000 with the object of reopening the railway from Appleby to Kirkby Stephen. In 2006 the section from Appleby to Warcop was reopened.

72

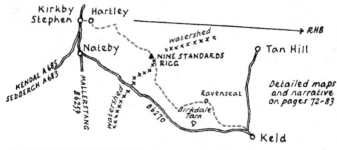

SECTION MAP: *KIRKBY STEPHEN to KELD: 12¾ miles*

This section has an important significance: on the top of Nine Standards Rigg the main Pennine watershed is crossed and Yorkshire entered. Thus far, all rivers and streams met have flowed to join the Irish Sea, west; beyond, they all flow to the North Sea, east. Thus far we have travelled *against* the grain, so to speak, but from here onwards we walk *with* the watercourses and to the same destination — but this doesn't mean it's now downhill all the way or that we have reached the halfway mark. Nevertheless, a quiet celebration on Nine Standards would not be out of place: at least there is no higher ground ahead on the journey.

At Keld we reach one of the major Yorkshire dales and the finest, Swaledale. Here too we collide, briefly, with the Pennine Way. Keld, famous for its waterfalls, is a small hamlet, a real outpost in the hills, but accommodation is restricted to one hotel and a few cottages.

The route recommended, over Nine Standards, traverses wild country, much of it pathless and without landmarks, and is not suitable for a wet or misty day. If there is a need to proceed regardless of bad weather, the quiet fell road leaving Nateby for Keld should be used instead: it is a motor road (B6270) but is almost traffic free except on summer Sundays. It reaches a height of 1698'. Note that in the event of the onset of bad weather on the Nine Standards route this road can be joined anywhere simply by walking south: it is unenclosed by fences across the top. It should also be borne in mind that, conversely, if the weather improves after a bad start, Nine Standards can be reached quickly from the summit of the road.

The B6270 is the sort of road, lonely and inhospitable, no more than a narrow thread of tarmac through barren hills, where a passing motorist feels an obligation to offer a lift to a solitary walker, especially one who seems inherently decent and is bravely struggling against the elements. If this happens you will decline, of course.

Kirkby Stephen

top:
The Parish Church
of St. Stephen

bottom:
Frank's Bridge

Hartley

KIRKBY STEPHEN to HARTLEY FELL

Leave Kirkby Stephen at the Market Square, taking a byway east to an old footbridge (Frank's Bridge) over the River Eden, where a path turns right along the river bank.

Here there are two alternatives. The quickest way is to continue along the path to Hartley: a charming village threaded by a stream and adorned with fine trees. At the road in Hartley, turn right and walk past houses. Look for a path on the left slanting down to a footbridge crossing Hartley Beck. Walk across the footbridge and turn right. Where the road bends sharp left, continue straight on and find a permissive footpath that passes behind Merrygill House to emerge onto the road. Turn right and follow the road uphill, passing the vast quarries, to its end after 1½ miles at a signpost pointing the bridleway to Rollinson Haggs, which follow. The views from this road are good and progress is fast.

A slightly longer but pleasanter alternative continues along the river where the path to Hartley leaves it. Then it roughly follows the valley of Ladthwaite Beck to the farm of Ladthwaite and continues along the farm drive. This alternative will please walkers to whom roads are an anathema and keeps to public footpaths throughout.

Nobody, however, should object to walking along the road from Hartley to the signpost: it is quiet, traffic-free, fringed with trees and gorse and poses no problems about the route — it gives a good start to the rough journey ahead. For these reasons it is given preference as the official route and mileage has been recorded on this map along it.

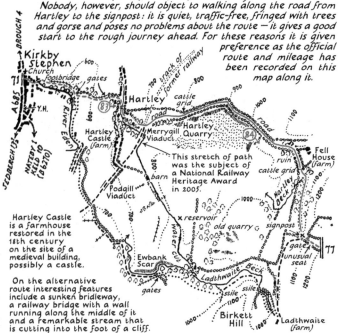

This stretch of path was the subject of a National Railway Heritage Award in 2005.

Hartley Castle is a farmhouse restored in the 18th century on the site of a medieval building, possibly a castle.

On the alternative route interesting features include a sunken bridleway, a railway bridge with a wall running along the middle of it and a remarkable stream that is cutting into the foot of a cliff.

There are many theories about the origin of the group of cairns long known as the Nine Standards, as is usually the case when the truth is not known. Certainly they are very old, appearing on 18th century maps and giving their name to the hill they adorn. The five northernmost cairns were rebuilt by master craftsman Steve Allen in 2005 and each has a different shape.

Nine Standards

They occupy a commanding position overlooking the Eden valley, this giving rise to the legend that they were built to give the marauding Scots the impression that an English army was encamped here. More likely they were boundary cairns (the county boundary formerly passed through them) or beacons. Harder to believe is the theory that the builders were local lads with nothing better to do to pass their time. Whatever their purpose, they were meant to endure, having suffered little from the storms of centuries.

The attainment of Nine Standards Rigg is an occasion for celebration. This is the main watershed of the walk and the most extensive and interesting viewpoint on it. Far back in the west is the skyline of Lakeland; the massifs of Cross Fell and Mickle Fell form the northern horizon, buttressing many miles of the Eden valley; in the south, much nearer, are the hills of Mallerstang and southeast is the promised land of Swaledale, fading into the haze of distance between the lofty portals of Great Shunner Fell and Rogan's Seat. Somewhere in that haze is the foot of our personal rainbow, journey's end.
If you are carrying a can of beer prepare to drink it now.

HARTLEY FELL to NINE STANDARDS RIGG

To minimise erosion in the area of Nine Standards Rigg, the Yorkshire Dales National Park signposts three different routes for use at different times of year. All three routes are shown on the maps below and on page 19.

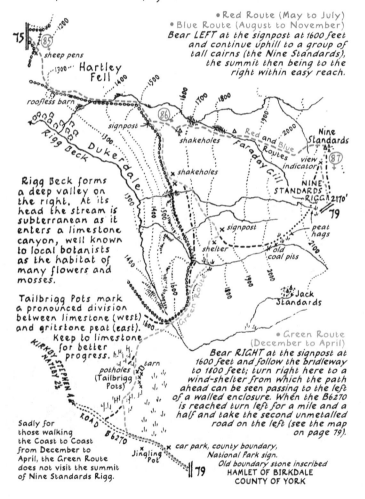

● Red Route (May to July)
● Blue Route (August to November)
Bear LEFT at the signpost at 1600 feet and continue uphill to a group of tall cairns (the Nine Standards), the summit then being to the right within easy reach.

Rigg Beck forms a deep valley on the right. At its head the stream is subterranean as it enters a limestone canyon, well known to local botanists as the habitat of many flowers and mosses.

Tailbrigg Pots mark a pronounced division between limestone (west) and gritstone peat (east). Keep to limestone for better progress.

● Green Route (December to April)
Bear RIGHT at the signpost at 1600 feet and follow the bridleway to 1800 feet; turn right here to a wind-shelter from which the path ahead can be seen passing to the left of a walled enclosure. When the B6270 is reached turn left for a mile and a half and take the second unmetalled road on the left (see the map on page 19).

Sadly for those walking the Coast to Coast from December to April, the Green Route does not visit the summit of Nine Standards Rigg.

car park, county boundary, National Park sign.
Old boundary stone inscribed HAMLET OF BIRKDALE COUNTY OF YORK

The summit of
White Mossy Hill,
looking to
Nine Standards Rigg

Whitsundale

The valley of Whitsundale bisects an upland wilderness
east of Nine Standards Rigg and winds its way down into
the lower reaches of Birkdale.   It is of considerable size
yet little known and rarely visited : it is deeply enclosed
by moors, is unseen from usual pedestrian tracks and
unsuspected from the only motor road in the vicinity. A
few farms occupy the entrance to the valley but beyond
Ravenseat all is desolation profound.

When our route reaches Ney Gill
we turn to enter Whitsundale at
Ravenseat and follow it down
to the Swale.

The pillar on
Millstones

NINE STANDARDS RIGG to WHITSUNDALE

• Red Route (May to July)
From Nine Standards Rigg aim south for the smooth grassy rise of White Mossy Hill, slightly east of south: a simple walk interrupted by peat hags in the depression between. Birkdale Tarn is now in view and gives the general direction of the long descent to Keld, but first head south to what appears to be a cairn but turns out to be a wind shelter. Now follows an exhilarating descent at a very easy gradient to a conspicuous stone pillar. During this descent the valley of Birkdale, threaded by the road to Keld, comes into view down on the right. When the path reaches an unmetalled road turn left.

• Red Route (May to July)
• Green Route (Dec. to April)
Continue along the valley of Ney Gill to the east.

77

NINE STANDARDS RIGG 2170'
× ruin

(88)

peat hags ┤ signposts

2100

2000

1900

main watershed of northern England

Blue Route
line of posts

1800 1700

× White Mossy Hill

Craygill Sike

fold

• Blue Route (Aug. to Nov.)
Head south from the summit and turn left at the second signpost. The route is marked by posts for most of its length, but it is difficult to follow because not every post is visible from the last. The path disappears at one point and resumes higher up the hill.

Red Route

2100

shelter

(89)

2000

wind shelter

This is the last 2000' contour crossed on the walk. Never again will we be so elevated.

1900

Coldberg Edge

1700

1600

Whitsundale Beck

pillar of stones

Millstones

1800

Coming down from Nine Standards Rigg the declining landscape engenders a feeling that the home stretch to R.H.B. has now been entered. Dispel it. We are not yet even halfway.

1800

1700

(90)

1600

1500

81

7

1600

1700

ROAD B6270

unmetalled roads

Birkdale Beck

KELD 4½

(91)

1500

fold ×

81

Green Route

Red and Green Routes
Ney Gill

shooting hut (a free-for-all shelter)

Ravenseat .... route -----

Footbridge,
Ravenseat

Waterfall,
Whitsundale
Bridge

79

Blue Route

Whitsundale Beck

1400

1400

• Ravenseat (farm)

gate

gate

waterfall

gate

79

Red and Green Routes

ruin

barn

barn

barns

Ney Gill   ford

1400

92

cattle grid

1400

ROAD to B6270

Cop Gill

1400

1500

gap

93

Caveside Gill

How Edge Scars (Boggle Hole)

barn

gate

Oven Mouth

1500

Eddy Fold

1300

1200

gate

below

Whitsundale Beck

Smithy Holme (derelict)

KIRKBY STEPHEN 9

1200

River Swale

ROAD B6270

• Blue Route (Aug. to Nov.)

Follow the path by Whitsundale Beck. When it ends, cross the fence and follow first a fence and then a wall to reach a ford where the three routes reunite.

• Red Route (May to July)
• Green Route (December to April)

The gentle descent by Ney Gill is uneventful, the track being generally easy to follow. All three routes reunite at the ford.

The path continues until an unmetalled road is joined, leading to the slender tarmac road to Ravenseat. Whitsundale Beck is crossed by going left along the road to Ravenseat, there using two bridges to reach the cottages up on the right, where a gate marks the start of a path along the eastern bank of the beck. Pleasant walking follows through walled pastures with gates and barns. The beck is always impressive, a fine waterfall being followed by a deep ravine into which there are dramatic peeps over the wall on its rim. When the path leaves the enclosures for the open fellside, keep on the same contour to pass below a large enclosure, Eddy Fold, which earns an Oscar as the biggest sheepfold ever seen. The farmhouse of Smithy Holme (derelict) now appears ahead.

Go down to it over marshy ground. A cart-track by the wall leads on past another disused farm and, a field further, becomes a lane descending to cross the River Swale and join the B6270.

Cotterby Scar

TAN HILL

1300

1200

1100

above

94

ruin

1100

1200

Wain Wath Force

ROAD B6270

Currack Force

Rainby Force

River Swale

1200

Catrake Force

1100

89

95

Keld

Keld Lodge

BEER 12

Preferably, instead of joining the B6270 at once, branch off the lane to the left in favour of a path along the limestone scar of Cotterby, using stiles in crosswalls and emerging on a hairpin bend of the Tan Hill road, which, followed to the right, soon joins the B6270. Keld is a long half-mile further.

Bed and breakfast is provided at Keld Lodge, which was once a Youth Hostel.

Keld.......

The little cluster of stone buildings at Keld, tidily yet haphazardly arranged along its only 'street', is attractively situated on a headland overlooking the Swale. Little has changed here for generations past, and proud dates and names of proud men adorn the doorways and walls and even the chapel belfry: a sundial records the hours but time is measured in centuries at Keld. This is the end of Swaledale —beyond are the wild moors of the watershed.

Cottages, farmsteads and innumerable barns starkly stand against a bleak and barren background. The joy of Keld is the Swale, a swift-flowing torrent sheltered by white cliffs of limestone fringed with trees and broken by falls and cataracts on its fast course from the desolate hills to the soft pastures of the valley.

Always, at Keld, there is the music of the river.

.... and some of its waterfalls

Wain Wath Force

KELD IS HALFWAY!

Catrake
Force

East Gill
Force

Kisdon
Force

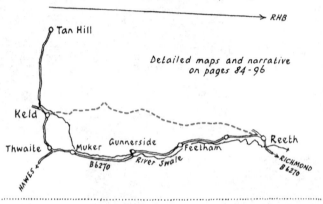

SECTION MAP : *KELD to REETH* : 11¼ *miles*

RHB

Tan Hill

Detailed maps and narrative on pages 84-96

Keld

Thwaite • Muker • Gunnerside • Feetham • Reeth

B6270 • River Swale

HAWES • RICHMOND B6270

For most walkers the royal road from Keld to Reeth will always be along the lovely banks of the Swale, the first three miles to Muker especially being very beautiful and the whole distance with minor interruptions being possible by using public footpaths on or near the riverside. If the day be wet or misty this is the way to go.

But the high-level route recommended in the following pages is of infinitely greater interest in addition to providing an excellent moorland walk made easy by the use of miners' tracks. The sites of several of the abandoned Swaledale lead mines are visited on the way, and, although they are now ruinous, enough remains to enable the imaginative visitor to reconstruct the scene as it used to be when thousands of men toiled here. They left their mark, and it is a dirty mark, so expect little of beauty in this section.

It is in this part of the walk, as our route aims from the hills for the valleys, that we pass from the settlements of the early Viking raiders, who found, in the mountainous northwest, country to their liking, a 'home from home', to those of the Danes, Angles and Saxons, who preferred the richer low ground to which, as tillers of the soil, they were accustomed.

It is almost possible to fix a boundary between the two types of settlement by reference to placenames only. *Keld* and *Thwaite* are pure Norse, as are the names of many natural features: *gill, fell, foss;* but as we proceed east to the gentler middle reaches of the valley, placenames ending in - *ton* (*Grinton, Fremington*) become frequent and are indicative of the Anglo-Saxon occupation, of which indeed there are visual evidences also in the terraced fields or lynchets seen here but absent in the uncultivated upper valley, where the Norsemen used the ground mainly for grazing. Earlier still were the Brigantes, who have also left their traces on the landscape. A few embossed pigs of lead have told of the Romans' interest in Swaledale, while an ancient fortification near Reeth dates back to prehistoric times. Over the ages Swaledale has been quite cosmopolitan; an influx of 'offcomers' is acquiring its barns and cottages for leisure pursuits. The natives remain impassive. They are accustomed to foreigners in Swaledale.

The route from Keld at once heads deep into the moors at Swinner Gill, from which it traverses high land to descend into Gunnerside Gill, a lonely graveyard of industrial relics, thence crossing a moorland devastated by spoil (where a secondary industry, of winning gravel, is now operating), after which it descends again to another mining area, and then skirts a more friendly fellside to reach Reeth, a pleasant and hospitable village with a choice of good hotels and private accommodation. There is a youth hostel across the river at nearby Grinton.

Swaledale

Lead Mining in Swaledale

In a search for information relating to the life and happenings of centuries ago one must often rely on imagination to fill in the details from the scanty evidences still remaining.

Not so in Swaledale. Anyone who wanders up the moors from the valley soon finds himself in the midst of a graphic scene of industrial decay that simply cannot be passed unnoticed. The gills, the fellsides, even the summits, have been torn asunder; shafts and levels pierce the earth like pockmarks; petrified rivers of stone litter the steep slopes; barren gullies make big scars in the heather; the skeletons of abandoned and derelict buildings stand gaunt and grey amid a chaos of spoil heaps. An observer of this dismal wreckage is left in no doubt that Swaledale has a long history of mining — and that this history has come to a full stop.

The date of the mines is uncertain. Most of them were opened in the 17th and 18th centuries but it is known that the Romans extracted lead here, probably from mines already existing, and that the Yorkshire monasteries owned workings. Later, a free-for-all developed, the landowners and men individually and in groups plundering the hills in search of profitable veins of ore. Another Klondyke arose in these wild hills. Thousands of men were engaged: a few 'struck it rich' but most toiled for little reward. Then, over the space of a decade towards the end of the 19th century, the industry collapsed. Not only were the best veins worked out but cheap foreign imports supplied the home demand. The population of Swaledale fell dramatically. Lead mining gave way to farming as the valley's source of prosperity.

In the triangle of land between Swaledale and Arkengarthdale particularly the scene even today is one of sterile devastation, despoliation, decay... There is no beauty in these sorry ruins but a great fascination for those of imagination who can picture in their minds the scene as it was a century before and still more for those who have the knowledge to piece together the fragments that remain.

There is a great need, before everything crumbles to dust, to preserve at least one of the mines as a site museum, not necessarily restoring the smelt and crushing mills and opening up the levels but reclaiming enough to demonstrate the methods of operation and the tools and equipment used, with a plan of the workings, graphs of annual output, and such supporting documentary records as may still be available. This could perhaps be done by one of the Universities or archaeological groups, and should be financed from Government funds.*

Our route takes us through the heart of the lead mining district yet gives only a faint insight of the vast area explored and exploited for ore. But note especially the Blakethwaite and Old Gang workings, which we pass, either one of which could be adapted for 20th century study and, it might well be hoped, for 20th century appreciation of the initiative, industry and ingenuity of men who lived hard, in times less favoured than those of today.

We have lost too much of the past through concern for the present.

* The ruins have now been stabilised so that no further deterioration can take place.

PRINCIPAL MINING AREAS IN SWALEDALE

This diagram indicates roughly the main areas extensively mined for lead, but in addition countless old shafts and levels, many of which proved abortive and were not fully developed, occur everywhere on the moors. The triangle of high ground between Arkengarthdale and Swaledale proved the most productive area, several square miles here being intensively worked — as is testified by today's sad scenery.

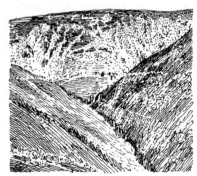

Swinner Gill

left:
   the approach

below left:
   the bridge

below right:
   Swinnergill Kirk

right:
   the ruins of the
   smelt mill, the
   waterfall, and
   the mine level
   at the foot of
   East Grain

KELD to SWINNERGILL MINES

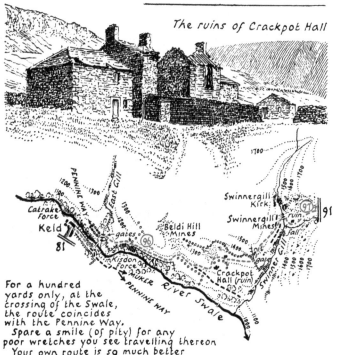

The ruins of Crackpot Hall

For a hundred yards only, at the crossing of the Swale, the route coincides with the Pennine Way.

Spare a smile (of pity) for any poor wretches you see travelling thereon Your own route is so much better

Leave Keld by a lane signposted to Muker. In 300 yards a path indicated by a Pennine Way signpost turns down left to reach a footbridge over the Swale, which cross and ascend the field opposite to a bridge above East Gill Force, in charming scenery. Here the Pennine Way turns left, our own route going across the gated bridge and continuing on a good cart-track to the sad ruins of Crackpot Hall, a once-handsome farmhouse (with a lovely view downriver to Muker) abandoned due to mining subsidence. Skirt the wall behind the ruins, passing a barn on another good track to arrive at a gate with an imposing view forward. Now a narrower path descends slightly, high above the deep rift of Swinner Gill, and, ignoring a branch left, reaches a fine bridge and the ruins of a smelting mill on the far bank, near a conspicuous waterfall with a mine-level adjacent. At this point Swinner Gill is left in favour of the branch-valley coming down from the east (East Grain), where a thin track ascends roughly along its north bank

Blakethwaite Smelt Mill

right:
  North Hush,
    from
  Bunton Hush

below:
  Gunnerside Gill

What is a hush?

A hush, in mining terms, is a ravine contrived by prospectors on a steep slope and is caused by the sudden release of water artificially dammed above it in such force as to strip the vegetation and scour the ground with the object of revealing any mineral content in the subsoil that might indicate the presence of a vein. (Today a bulldozer would be used.) These hushes are found in many mining districts and are especially conspicuous in Gunnerside Gill.

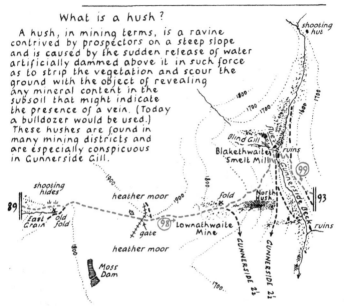

When the gradient alongside East Grain eases, the track becomes indistinct on wet ground near a sheepfold, but the route soon joins a gravel road, which crosses the top of the moor. The walking here, across dark heather moorland, is excellent, with far-reaching views to be enjoyed. At the highest point (1895') there is a glimpse of Moss Dam, an interesting relic of mining days crossed by a causeway. After passing a small enclosure the road crosses the fence that marks the boundary between the parishes of Muker and Melbecks. As the road descends it passes through an area of mining debris, and, beyond a sheepfold, turns down to the right (for Gunnerside). Just before the bend a number of cairns on the left mark the start of the path to be taken. Before long, a great disturbance of the ground on the right indicates the natural but man-inspired ravine of North Hush. In a quarter of a mile turn sharp right and then left along a good track to the imposing remains of the Blakethwaite Smelt Mill, where the beck is crossed by a huge stone slab to a cloister-like ruin. The fine arched entrance in the illustration has gone, but the smaller arches are still there. Looking back, note the flue coming straight down the rough fellside from a notch in the skyline and the well-preserved kiln to its right. Now ascend the zigzags to a green path and follow it to the right.

Level House Bridge

Old Gang
Smell Mill

GUNNERSIDE MINES to SURRENDER BRIDGE

The path along the east bank of Gunnerside Beck arrives suddenly at a remarkable area of devastation, a succession of hushes having gouged out much of the fellside ahead. Do not descend with the path to the plentiful remains of mining activity in the bottom of the gill but slant half-left over the stony wastes, climbing steadily across the hushes to a post with a yellow arrow, where a track from Gunnerside is joined. A cairn and a post embedded in a cairn show the way to go. Now follows a surprising tract of ground: on the top of the moor ahead all vegetation has been destroyed by a deep covering of gravel, the spoil of old mines and pits. Although the altitude reaches 1863', nothing less like a Yorkshire moor can be imagined.

100 miles! Yippee!!

Old Gang Mines

For a third of a mile not a blade of grass nor a sprig of heather is seen, the natural moorland having been transformed into an arid desert of stone. The spoil here is being reclaimed, and, incongruously, tractors may be met. Whether or not one approves of the ravaging of natural scenery on so vast a scale, the access roadway for vehicles leading down to the valley ahead is a great boon for foot-travellers, who can make rapid progress along it and are spared the slow and wearying trudge over rough ground to which they would be committed without its help. On the descent, if the day be clear, there is a first glimpse of the Cleveland Hills far ahead.

The vehicle roadway descends easily to a bridge and continues down the valley, passing an interesting group of mine buildings and a mill chimney. If not delayed by inspections of these relics, Surrender Bridge will be reached in fine style at a speed of four m.p.h.

A : to FEETHAM
B : to HEALAUGH

Smelt Mill, Surrender Bridge

Calver Hill

Cross the tarmac just above Surrender Bridge and continue on a signposted footpath downstream to the sad ruin of a smelt mill, unchanged since it was illustrated. Here bear half-left across a heather moor, wet in places. Aim for the left edge of a field seen ahead.

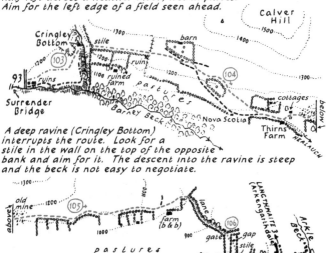

A deep ravine (Cringley Bottom) interrupts the route. Look for a stile in the wall on the top of the opposite bank and aim for it. The descent into the ravine is steep and the beck is not easy to negotiate.

Scramble up the grassy east bank to the stile (found near a junction of walls): it is of the narrow 'squeeze through' type and will pose a grave problem for walkers with bow legs. But thenceforward all is plain sailing on an enjoyable 'high-level' path. From the stile keep above the intake wall to a ruinous barn, where continue in the same direction, passing a walled enclosure on the left. At the far end of the enclosure bear right and then bear left, passing to the left of another enclosure, and slanting down to a farm, Thirns. Here turn briefly uphill, left, to pass in front of a cottage, Moorcock. Note the two barns thatched with heather, one above the cottage, the other on the far side of the green. Now follow a gravel road through an area of spoil, continuing forward above intake walls on the same contour. When the road bends left near a farm carry straight on along a grass path to a gated lane that descends between walls to the B6270, the last section being short-cut in fields to reach the road by a ginnel alongside a school. Turn left to Reeth. The views in the course of this walk are excellent.

Reeth

Reeth, as befits its proud title as the 'capital' of upper Swaledale, occupies a strategic point of vantage on an open hillside overlooking the confluence of Arkle Beck and the Swale. Here the deep trench of Arkengarthdale, which seems destined to bear forever the gaunt scars of its abandoned mining industry, loses its identity in the more verdant and lovelier main valley.

Reeth is a pleasant place, its buildings forming a square around a large green that is gay with daffodils in springtime but littered on summer weekends with coaches and cars and too many human beings. Once primarily concerned with mining and housing twice its present population Reeth today is mainly engaged in catering for a growing influx of tourists and supplying the needs of the valley communities: there are many hotels and shops and a museum. Notably absent is the parish church: this, 'the cathedral of Swaledale', is situated a mile away across the River Swale at Grinton. Reeth is, in fact, distant from the river, and is more intimately concerned with Arkle Beck, itself a considerable watercourse, which forms the eastern boundary of the village.

No railway ever penetrated the upper reaches of Swaledale — what a scenic journey it would have provided, what a pageant of beauty! — but a few buses pass through Reeth daily, linking Richmond and Keld.

A corner of Reeth

SECTION MAP : REETH to RICHMOND : 10½ miles

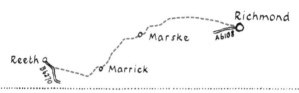

→ RHB

Detailed maps and narrative
on pages 97·109

Richmond

Marske

Reeth

Marrick

B6270

A6108

This section is short and easily accomplished, but is so abundantly endowed with variety and beauty and interest that it would be unforgivable to rush it in half a day; one should arrange nevertheless to finish with an hour or two to spare for an inspection of Richmond's many historical buildings. The scenery throughout this section is of high quality, with the Swale the dominant feature and lovely everywhere. The river may be followed more closely than the route given, but it is preferable to keep high along the hillsides and so enjoy quieter walking and extensive views. This the recommended route does.

REETH to MARRICK PRIORY

Take the Richmond road out of Reeth, leaving it when it turns south at Fremington and continuing along the Marske by-road for a further half-mile to a left-hand bend where a narrow metalled road goes straight on. Proceed along the narrow road in pleasant surroundings, the lovely river and valley scenery being marred only by the presence of caravans. The Swale has grown fat since we last saw it at Keld.

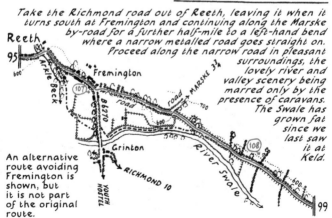

Reeth
95
600

Arkle Beck

Fremington

107

B6270

road

road

MARSKE 3½

700

Grinton

RICHMOND 10

YOUTH HOSTEL

108

River Swale

600

An alternative route avoiding Fremington is shown, but it is not part of the original route.

99

Marrick Priory

Marrick Priory was established in the 12th century and occupied by Benedictine nuns until it was dissolved by Henry VIII It became a sad ruin except for the tower but some restoration has been undertaken, and new buildings added for use as an adventure centre.

Marrick Priory is in ruins except for the tower, and partly concealed by new buildings occupied by the Ripon Diocese as an adventure centre and the barns and byres of Abbey Farm adjacent. Note the realistic model owl perched on a farm building on the right.

At this point leave the farm road in favour of a grass path slanting up to a wicket-gate giving entrance into a wood. A flagged path leads upwards alongside a wall: a delightful interlude, the way being edged by floriferous banks. (This path through the wood is known as Nunnery Steps, and is reputed to have 375 steps, but they are insignificant, not like a stairway). The path emerges into a field, reaching a gate and continuing between a chapel and a church, both of which have now been converted into houses. They serve as portals to the small hamlet of Marrick beyond and they doubtless give an exaggerated impression of the former religious fervour of its few inhabitants. (The village post office, inn, school and smithy have also been converted into houses.) In the village turn right at a telephone box and right again at a Coast to Coast sign. When the tarmac ends bear left and keep straight on through a succession of little gates. The view ahead now opens up considerably, Hutton's Monument being conspicuous on the line of march. The route now descends to Eller Beck (which undergoes three changes of name in three miles), crossing an unnecessary stile and a farm road and maintaining a beeline indicated by gates and stiles to the house of Ellers, a charming 'conversion' remarkable by its lack of an access road. Pass round the house to a wooden footbridge and, ascending slightly, aim across the next field diagonally to a gate and continue in the same direction through another.

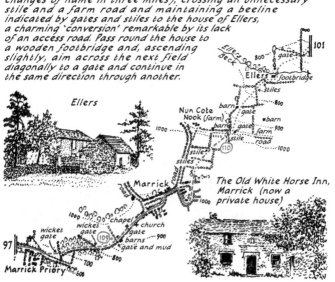

101

Eller Beck   gate.

Ellers   footbridge

stiles

800

Nun Cote   barn   gate
Nook (farm)   barn   •barn
1000   barn   gate   900
   farm
110   stile   road
   1000

stile
stiles

Ellers

Marrick

1000

The Old White Horse Inn, Marrick (now a private house)

1000   chapel   church
wicket   gate
gate   900
109   barns
   gate and mud
wicket
gate
97
Marrick Priory   800
700
600

Marske.........

...Hall

...Church

...Bridge

The path from Ellers reaches the farm road to Hollins alongside a plantation. The right of way, straight ahead, is now interrupted by a wire fence, which can be negotiated by a stile on the right. Continue alongside a well-built wall (the boundary of the former deer park of Marske Hall), crossing the fence again to a gap on the right, from where a slanting course across a field leads to the Reeth–Marske road, reached by a stile opposite a bungalow. In splendid scenery, go down the road to Marske Bridge (where there is a Coast to Coast sign in the middle of the triangle) and up the hill to the hamlet of Marske.

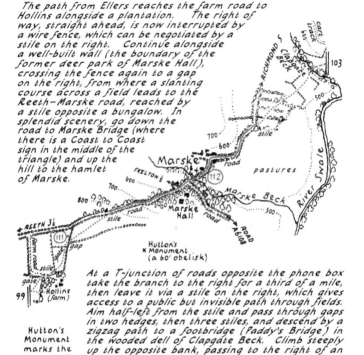

Hutton's Monument marks the grave of Matthew Hutton (1814)

At a T-junction of roads opposite the phone box take the branch to the right for a third of a mile, then leave it via a stile on the right, which gives access to a public but invisible path through fields. Aim half-left from the stile and pass through gaps in two hedges, then three stiles, and descend by a zigzag path to a footbridge (Paddy's Bridge) in the wooded dell of Clapgate Beck. Climb steeply up the opposite bank, passing to the right of an electricity pole. From the fence corner aim for a slender white cairn where the route joins a good cart-track contouring the slope above.

Marske

Marske lies snugly sequestered amongst fine trees in a side valley of Swaledale, a glacial fold in the hills, fringed by limestone cliffs with wild heathery moors beyond. The charm of the place is its natural scenery but the lovely grounds of Marske Hall contribute to the richness of the landscape. The Hall was for centuries the home of the distinguished Hutton family, producing two Archbishops of York, but is now occupied as flats following a sale of the estate. Also worthy of mention is the 12th century church of St. Edmund, retaining some of its original features and interesting later additions.

High Applegarth
and Whitcliffe Scar
(now converted into
private houses)

Whitcliffe Wood

CLAPGATE BECK to WHITCLIFFE WOOD

The cart-track is the access road for West Applegarth Farm. It occupies a pleasant shelf below a limestone cliff and has a lovely view of the Swale in its wooded valley and of the rolling foothills around Marske, Hutton's Monument being prominent. Go east along it, passing a bank of yew, to the farm, where it ends. The clue to further progress is the wall corner ahead, where a tiny gate indicates

the way to go. In a hundred yards, where the route is clear, there is a Coast to Coast signpost. Keeping on the same contour the route continues over two pastures, crosses the drive to Low Applegarth and merges with the drive to East Applegarth, leaving it by a stile on the left. Before long a path on the right leads to the camping barn at East Applegarth. The scenery hereabouts is pleasant, having the stony slopes of Whitcliffe Scar high on the left — note the monument commemorating Willance's Leap on the skyline — and the richly wooded valley of the Swale, its only disfigurement being a caravan site, down on the right. The way ahead is now distinct, the path becoming a farm-road entering Whitcliffe Wood and bound for Richmond.

Willance's Leap

Whitcliffe Scar and Wood is a popular local walk, the best-known feature being the spot known as Willance's Leap. This is not a spectacular precipice, as the name might suggest, and would attract no attention were it not associated with an occurrence in 1606 when Robert Willance fell down the steep slope here while riding, his horse being killed. Robert was unharmed and, grateful for his deliverance, gave to the town of Richmond as a thankoffering a silver chalice, preserved to this day as one of the town's many treasures.

RICHMOND

MAP OF TOWN CENTRE
AND FEATURES OF INTEREST

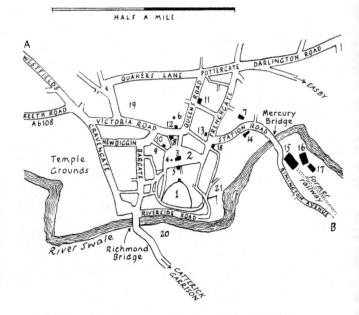

HALF A MILE

1 : Castle Ruins
2 : Market Place
3 : Holy Trinity Church
4 : Market Cross
5 : Town Hall
6 : Grey Friars' Tower
7 : St. Mary's Parish Church
8 : Georgian Theatre
9 : Finkle Street
10 : General Post Office

11 : Public Library
12 : Tourist Information
13 : Richmondshire Museum
14 : Richmond School
15 : Cinema (former station)
16 : Swimming Pool
17 : Health Club
18 : Council Offices
19 : Cricket Ground
20 : Football Ground

21 : Waterfalls

A : Point of entry of route into the town
B : Point of departure

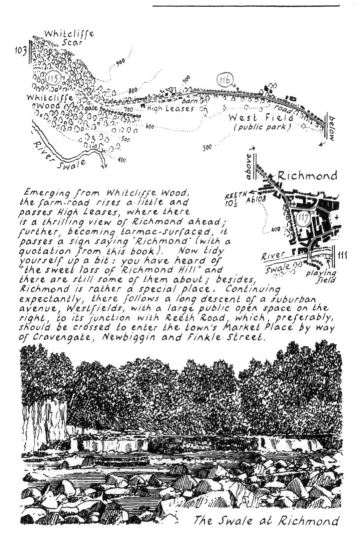

Emerging from Whitcliffe Wood,
the farm-road rises a little and
passes High Leases, where there
is a thrilling view of Richmond ahead;
further, becoming tarmac-surfaced, it
passes a sign saying 'Richmond' (with a
quotation from this book). Now tidy
yourself up a bit: you have heard of
"the sweet lass of Richmond Hill" and
there are still some of them about; besides,
Richmond is rather a special place. Continuing
expectantly, there follows a long descent of a suburban
avenue, Westfields, with a large public open space on the
right, to its junction with Reeth Road, which, preferably,
should be crossed to enter the town's Market Place by way
of Cravengate, Newbiggin and Finkle Street.

The Swale at Richmond

Richmond

Richmond is a town unlike others, a place unique, rich in relics of the past, steeped in a long history that still lingers in the ramifications of its castle and the narrow alleys and quaint buildings that huddle in the shelter of the massive Norman keep. The castle, dramatically poised on a cliff high above the Swale, is the dominating feature, but hardly less impressive is the large cobbled market place with the ancient church of the Holy Trinity rising from the stones and now housing the Green Howards Museum, or the fine tower standing amid the ruins of a Friary. Other buildings also have associations with days gone by, notably the restored Georgian Theatre and Richmond School, where Lewis Carroll was once a pupil. Many of the streets, too, have an atmosphere of antiquity, happily preserved in their names, and picturesque corners abound. It is a town of reminders of times long past. Richmond folk have always jealously guarded their heritage and consequently the town centre shows little in the nature of 20th century 'improvements' : their reward for vigilance and a recognition of true values is a romantic town that has 'gloriously defied time' and today looks very much as it has done for many centuries past. The British Council recently selected Richmond as the typical English market town; but in its resistance of the sort of modern development to which other market towns have largely succumbed it has earned a better compliment than 'typical'. Unique, yes.

Richmond has long been associated with the military, a traditional connection greatly emphasised by a series of extensions to the nearby Catterick Camp, which has grown into one of the largest military establishments in England. Catterick Camp has become a town in itself, larger in area than Richmond: a vast complex of barracks and dwellings and administrative offices supplemented by many shopping arcades and religious and recreational facilities. But its ties, socially and economically, with the mother town, stay strong. Catterick is the garrison, Richmond the garrison town.

Richmond, with a population of around 8500, is the only town (begging Kirkby Stephen's pardon) visited on our route. It is too good to be by-passed.

The Castle Keep

A Richmond
Portfolio

Castle Walk

Holy Trinity Church
Market Place

Waterfalls
on the Swale

Grey Friars' Tower

The Georgian Theatre

Dogs' Toilet
on the river bank
(no longer in use)

Richmond Bridge

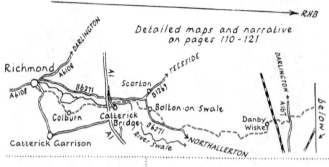

SECTION MAP : *RICHMOND to INGLEBY CROSS* : 23 *miles*

→ RHB

Detailed maps and narrative on pages 110 - 121

If you are fond of placid rural scenery and have an interest in farming, you might enjoy this section of the walk; but if your preference is for high ground and rough hills you will find it tedious.

This crossing from Swaledale to the Cleveland Hills is the only section of the route that lies wholly over low ground. There is no escape to uncultivated heath or moorland even briefly. On the Ordnance Survey map 'hills' and 'moors' are plentiful but these place-names are misleading: note instead the contours, which nowhere rise even to a paltry 300 feet. Here is a twenty-mile gap, a fertile plain little above the sea: it is the northern extension of the Vale of York and known locally as the Vale of Mowbray — and there is no way of bridging it. Rich it is, in farming terms, much of it being arable with barley as the main crop, and quite unspoilt. In 1973, when this guide first appeared, the area was seldom visited by tourists and the author found many paths had fallen into disuse. He advised taking to the country lanes instead, to cover the ground as quickly as possible. These days, however, almost the whole distance can be covered on footpaths and bridleways over which the public has the right to pass, and paths are no longer difficult to follow. In all probability the route described here is the one originally intended.

Accommodation is available in Danby Wiske and at Lovesome Hill Farm, half a mile north of Oaktree Hill. Failing that, there is a bus route from Oaktree Hill to Northallerton, where much accommodation is available.

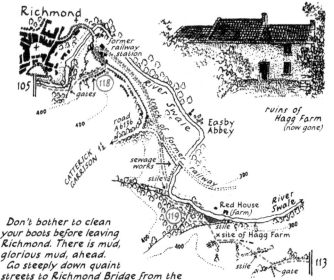

Richmond

former railway station

105

gates

118

400

400

road A6136

River Swale

track of former railway

CATTERICK 1½

sewage works

stile

Easby Abbey

ruins of Hagg Farm (now gone)

railway

300

Red House (farm)

119

site of Hagg Farm

River Swale

300

stile

400

stile

gate

113

Don't bother to clean your boots before leaving Richmond. There is mud, glorious mud, ahead.

Go steeply down quaint streets to Richmond Bridge from the southwest corner of the Market Place, cross it, and take the path downriver on the south bank past a playing field. After passing through a wood and crossing a field, take the gate on the right, passing between farm buildings and in front of ten semi-detached houses (Priory Villas) to reach the A6136. Go left along this for 200 yards and turn sharp right along the side of the old railway station. Follow the disused railway line for half a mile, then turn right over a cattle grid and immediately left, passing a sewage works, which contrasts incongruously with the noble ruins of Easby Abbey, well seen across the river. After 200 yards, keep to the right of the works fence along the base of a grassy bank to a stile into a wood with the Swale now alongside. A path leads through the wood by the river's edge (this is where your boots get mucky again) to a wooden footbridge over a side-stream when it ascends among the trees and runs along the top of a cliff to a stile in a fence. Here the path passes through gorse bushes and comes to the site of Hagg Farm, where one tiny building survives. A cart track leads away to the left, but after the first field the right of way leaves it. Now follow closely the map above. The path is unclear and there are no landmarks to steer by, but there is confirmation of the 'official' route into Colburn provided by two stiles in quick succession, a kissing gate and a Coast to Coast signpost.

The old village of Colborn (there is a large modern estate of houses nearby, but out of sight) is entered by the side of a beck, too deep and wide to ford but avoided by a path on the left, which emerges into a lane: at its end cross the green via a crossroads and a bridge to the village street, which has an inn, the Hildyard Arms.

Ordnance Survey maps show two bridleways to the east from Colborn, but the more northerly of them no longer exists in its initial stages along the line shown on Ordnance maps owing to subsidence. Turn right at a Coast to Coast signpost and left at another. On the left are some farm buildings with unusual features that have been converted into houses. When the road bends left go straight on along a cart track, turning left at the end of the second field to join the other bridleway. It runs pleasantly east with the wooded banks of the Swale on the left. A continuous noise starts to assail the ears on this section: the sound of traffic on the A1, a mile ahead. A fence is crossed (gate and stile) beyond which the bridleway becomes less distinct but trend slightly right to join the access road to S.t Giles Farm at another gate. The outbuildings of S.t Giles Farm have been converted into houses and replaced by modern farm buildings. Leave the road after 100 yards to follow a wire fence on the left along the top of the wooded bank of the Swale. Two long fields forward a fenced lane is entered to reach Thornbrough Farm. By this time the din of the A1 has risen to a crescendo, and suddenly there it is just ahead and unexpectedly below eye-level, crossing the Swale on a bridge with no architectural merit. Go steeply down to the river, pass under the bridge and then another carrying a disused railway. Turn immediately right and right again up some steps to join the railway. Cross over the river and follow it to the right to the north end of Catterick Bridge, near the site of CATARACTONIUM, a Roman town, but dominated today by a modern racecourse.

Go straight on and continue along the river bank, becoming accompanied by an ancient buttressed wall thought to be a Roman embankment. When the path ends continue following the river until you come to a pair of gates. Go through the left-hand gate and follow the path ahead to join a fenced lane close to its junction with the B6271. Turn right along the lane and then left along another lane with Bolton-on-Swale church straight ahead in trees.

Catterick Bridge

Colburn Hall, seen off route on the left, is an interesting rebuilt Tudor mansion with a separate Manor Hall nearby.

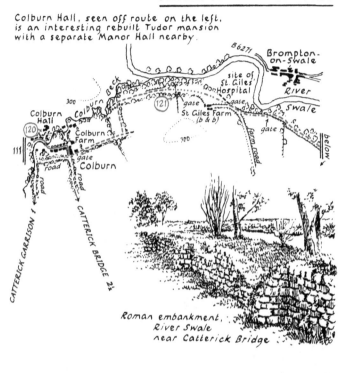

Roman embankment, River Swale near Catterick Bridge

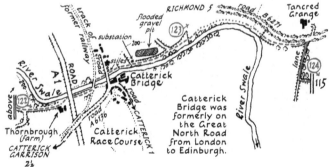

Catterick Bridge was formerly on the Great North Road from London to Edinburgh.

114

The Jenkins Memorial,
St. Mary's Churchyard,
Bolton-on-Swale.

Believe it or not,
Henry Jenkins was born
at Ellerton-on-Swale in
the year 1500 and died
there in 1670 at the
age of 169.
This monument
was erected by public
contribution in 1743 to
commemorate his long
life: a well-deserved
recognition of
a remarkable
achievement.

St. Mary's Church,
Bolton-on-Swale

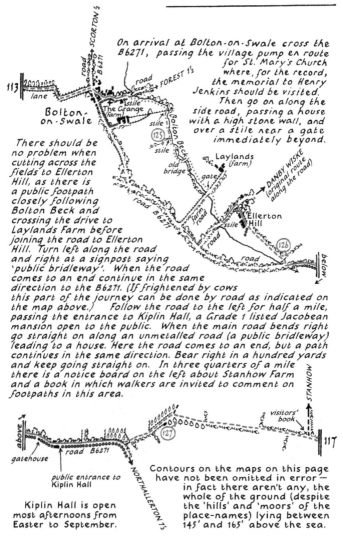

On arrival at Bolton·on·Swale cross the B6271, passing the village pump en route for St. Mary's Church where, for the record, the memorial to Henry Jenkins should be visited. Then go on along the side road, passing a house with a high stone wall, and over a stile near a gate immediately beyond.

There should be no problem when cutting across the fields to Ellerton Hill, as there is a public footpath closely following Bolton Beck and crossing the drive to Laylands Farm before joining the road to Ellerton Hill. Turn left along the road and right at a signpost saying 'public bridleway'. When the road comes to an end continue in the same direction to the B6271. (If frightened by cows this part of the journey can be done by road as indicated on the map above.)   Follow the road to the left for half a mile, passing the entrance to Kiplin Hall, a Grade 1 listed Jacobean mansion open to the public. When the main road bends right go straight on along an unmetalled road (a public bridleway) leading to a house. Here the road comes to an end, but a path continues in the same direction. Bear right in a hundred yards and keep going straight on. In three quarters of a mile there is a notice board on the left about Stanhow Farm and a book in which walkers are invited to comment on footpaths in this area.

Kiplin Hall is open most afternoons from Easter to September.

Contours on the maps on this page have not been omitted in error — in fact there aren't any, the whole of the ground (despite the 'hills' and 'moors' of the place-names) lying between 145' and 165' above the sea.

To walkers whose liking is for high places and rough terrain, this will seem the dullest part of the whole walk; those who believe the earth is flat will be mightily encouraged on this section. The scenery is 100% rural, and all is tidily and pleasantly arranged, but views are restricted to the route and the fields adjoining : there is no distance to attract the eye, no stimulating prospect apart from the faraway outline of the Cleveland Hills, too remote yet to excite. You have heard of Yorkshire's broad acres: here they are in person, interminably, neatly patterned by clipped thorn hedges or wooden fences, but hardly ever a stone wall: a foreign land indeed. Happily all the roads that are utilised are provided

with ample grass verges that are kinder to the feet than the tarmac, but tedium grows apace and one plods onwards mechanically, head down, thinking nostalgically of places left behind : Lakeland, limestone country, the Dales. Although in the midst of a thriving husbandry, few people are seen; in fact, one feels lonelier here than one does on the mountains. There is nothing to see, nothing worthy of illustration, nothing of interest to anyone but farmers. Danby Wiske is the only village and less attractive than its name. At 110 feet above the sea, it is the lowest point between the coastal extremities of the walk.

Half a mile past the visitors' book the path comes to a public road, but just before this is reached turn sharp left along a farm road leading to Red House (which is not red). At the end of the farm buildings turn right, and at Moor House follow the arrows to the right of all the outbuildings. Continue in the same direction until you come to a road. Then turn right, and left along the drive to High Brockholme. When the drive bends

right go straight on along a public footpath. The first two gates are padlocked, but the fences to the left of them are climbable. At the third gate turn left and then right. In a quarter of a mile the path becomes hedged on both sides and is very pleasant to walk along. When the hedge on your right-hand side ends continue to follow the path along the edge of the field until you come to a road, and turn left. The Ordnance Survey map shows a moat here, but it can't be seen from the road.

Danby Wiske Church

The road leads into Danby Wiske (where accommodation is available and meals are provided at the White Swan Inn). Turn right in the village, and about a mile later take a public footpath on the left leading to Oaktree Hill.

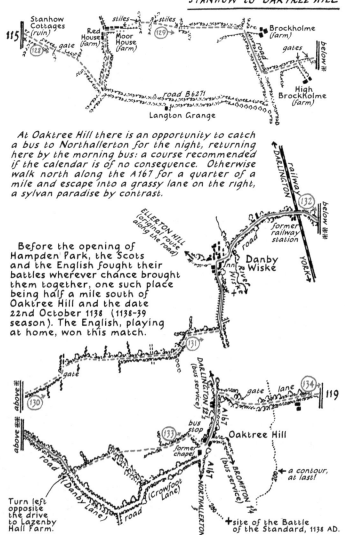

At Oaktree Hill there is an opportunity to catch a bus to Northallerton for the night, returning here by the morning bus: a course recommended if the calendar is of no consequence. Otherwise walk north along the A167 for a quarter of a mile and escape into a grassy lane on the right, a sylvan paradise by contrast.

Before the opening of Hampden Park, the Scots and the English fought their battles wherever chance brought them together, one such place being half a mile south of Oaktree Hill and the date 22nd October 1138 (1138-39 season). The English, playing at home, won this match.

Turn left opposite the drive to Lazenby Hall Farm.

Harlsey Grove
as it appeared in 1972

Rights of Way

A right of way is defined as a "right established by usage to pass over another's land".

Public roads are dedicated for the use of the public at large, on wheels or on foot, and are therefore rights of way unless prohibition is imposed on specified forms of progression (pedestrians on motorways, for example) by the highway authorities.

Private roads, including most farm access roads, have no rights of way unless such are established by use and recorded on the footpath maps maintained by the local authorities for the district

Access land may be freely wandered over by all.

What are more usually referred to as walkers' rights of way are *public footpaths* and *bridleways* over private land. Such rights may be legally provided in title deeds or they may simply have developed by the tread of feet over a period so long that "the memory of man runneth not to the contrary". Where rights of way do exist it is incumbent upon the owner or tenant to permit through access by means of stiles or gates and keep the route free from hazard. Where a public footpath is in general use these conditions are invariably observed, but where little or no use is made of rights of way by the public there is a natural tendency to disregard their existence and cease to maintain them. This was formerly the situation in the section from Richmond to Ingleby Cross, where footpaths were frequently not only invisible on the ground but often found to be blocked by obstructions, including bulls.

The difficulties and hazards experienced by the author in negotiating the rights of way incorporated in this section of the route were reported in gruesome detail to the North Riding County Council, who kindly undertook a survey, as the result of which a smoother passage can be enjoyed by present-day travellers.

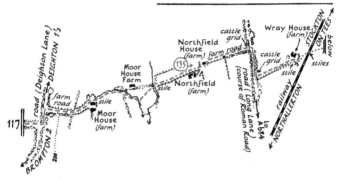

The grassy lane debouches into a road (Deighton Lane). This road can be followed north by those, if any, addicted to road-walking, taking a branch road east and so rejoining the direct route at the far end of Low Moor Lane. But the direct route as shown on these maps, following rights of way across country, is not only pleasanter but saves a mile in distance if nothing in time. From Deighton Lane take the drive to Moor House, keeping left of all farm buildings. When you reach Long Lane turn right, and then left along the drive to Wray House. At the start of the farmyard turn right, noting the realistic model rats on the stile. Then cut across the pasture to the step-stile in the railway fence. There is a concrete bridge over Ing Beck, and at Harlsey Grove the path is diverted to the right in order to avoid the farmyard.

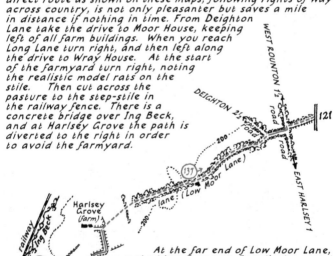

At the far end of Low Moor Lane, cross the West Rounton - East Harlsey road and enter, between imposing gateposts, the farm-road-cum-drive almost opposite: this is the approach to Sydal Lodge, ahead amid trees, and is also a right of way.

Brecken Hill

now just a pile of rubble....

Ingleby Arncliffe

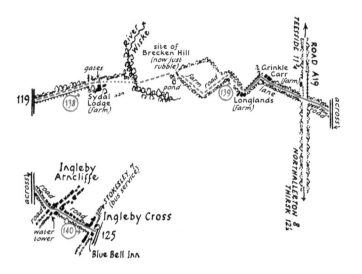

On the approach to Sydal Lodge the Cleveland Hills are seen clearly ahead, the contraption on the skyline being a British Telecom microwave radio station, useful as a guide to the start of the long tramp over the moors to the North Sea, positively the last stage of the walk.

Sydal Lodge is almost hidden in fine trees. Pass alongside farm buildings and straight on down a field to a footbridge over the sluggish River Wiske (the same stream we saw at Danby, being destined to meander aimlessly and hopelessly around the countryside in a vain search for a contour that would give it an objective). From the footbridge follow the path to the pond and the rubble of Brecken Hill (once a pig farm). Here join an improving cart-track that winds along past the farms of Longlands and Grinkle Carr to reach the tumult of the very busy dual carriageway of the A19 road. Crossing this race track is the final hazard of the day: summon up the last vestiges of energy to scurry across at top speed into the calm of a byroad leading to the pleasant village of Ingleby Arncliffe (with its unusual Arts and Crafts water tower), whence it continues downhill to Ingleby Cross.

Accommodation and food may be booked or available at the Blue Bell Inn; bed-and-breakfast accommodation is also to be found in both Ingleby Arncliffe and Ingleby Cross.

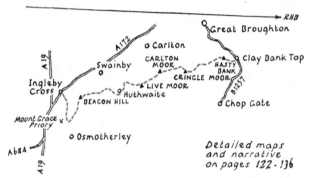

SECTION MAP : *INGLEBY CROSS to CLAY BANK TOP* : 12¼ miles

*Detailed maps
and narrative
on pages 122-136*

This is the finest section of our marathon (outside Lakeland) a splendid high-level traverse along the escarpment of the Cleveland Hills: beautiful country with far-reaching views.

The path from Beacon Hill onwards is (thanks to Lyke Wake walkers) blazed almost as wide as a road, and, with signs at the few points of doubt, only a genius could go astray. The problem here is not route-finding but accommodation at the end of the day, a matter fully discussed on page 136, and it may well be advisable to ring ahead for a bed before leaving Ingleby Cross, having considered the weather, the hours of daylight and one's personal prowess, if any, as a resolute walker.

This is the start of the long crossing of the North York Moors and he will enjoy it most who has read about them in advance. A few notes are appended but are no substitute for books and websites created by those with greater knowledge of the area. For 18 miles our route follows the line of the Lyke Wake Walk, including 12 that also coincide with the Cleveland Way. Much has been written about both these long-distance pedestrian routes and the Long Distance Walkers Assoc. website (www.ldwa.org.uk) is well worth a visit.

*The Blue Bell Inn
Ingleby Cross*

For general reading, *Discover the North York Moors* by Roger Osbourne, the official guide to the National Park, is recommended.

The North York Moors

The broad expanse of moorland extending for 30 miles from the Vale of Mowbray to the east coast, heatherclad, unenclosed, uninhabited, remote from industry and noise and free from traffic, is a magnificent territory for the walker: open country like the Pennines and the Cheviots yet more handsome and colourful — and friendlier by far. It is a wilderness crossed by few roads but many ancient tracks, a plateau high above the valleys yet of sleek and rounded slopes and easy gradients, where one can wander tirelessly all day and enjoy freedom complete; an elevated desert neither arid nor sterile but abounding in interest and beauty. And not only the walker will find a delight here. For the archaeologist, the searcher after objects ancient, the moors tell the story of the primitive people who settled here in ages past when climatic conditions for a time were kinder and the hills, then wooded, served both as home and hunting ground: their cairns and earthworks, barrows and burial mounds remain to this day remarkably profuse; of the Romans who flitted across the scene briefly leaving little of present interest excepting a road, recently partially restored, and signal stations; of Scandinavian invaders who, later, first set the patterns of community life that have survived; most of the village names have a Norse or Danish origin. The botanist and naturalist, the geologist and mineralogist, are all catered for on the wild hills and in the sheltered valleys. Today it is hard to believe that these uplands were formerly exploited for the wealth below the surface, but in fact they have been worked extensively for iron and coal, and, distinctively, for jet and alum. These industries are now all abandoned and nature is hiding their traces although the tracks of the mineral railways, the iron workings and jet spoilheaps are likely to be permanent reminders. A potash mine has been set up in the National Park employing 800 people, and forestry operations have spread along the hillsides; quite incongruous in an area remarkable for its prehistoric relics is an ultra-modern Ballistic Missile Early Warning Station.

The geographical boundaries of the area are clearly defined by a surround of valleys. To the north is Teesside; to the west is the Vale of Mowbray, to the south is the Vale of Pickering and the eastern boundary is the coastal strip: all lowlying land, and in their midst rises quite sharply the high plateau with its backbone on a west-east axis and of remarkably consistent altitude but indented by deep valleys, longer in the south where the slopes are gentler than they are northwards. Separating the valleys are high ridges. Each valley has its stream, feeding one of three main rivers: the Esk (north), the Rye and the Derwent (south).

The absence of walls and fences gives a rare feeling of freedom to expeditions 'over the tops' and two long-distance pedestrian routes have become increasingly popular. One is the Lyke Wake Walk, an arduous 40-mile tramp having a time limit of 24 hours; the other is the 100-mile marathon known as the Cleveland Way. With both, as instigator of one and supporter of the other, the name of Bill Cowley is indelibly associated.

ANCIENT.......

The Church,
Mount Grace
Priory

Mount Grace Priory

Dating from 1398, Mount Grace Priory is one of the best surviving examples of the few Carthusian foundations in this country. The monks lived here in seclusion, almost as hermits, each isolated in his own cell with a garden, observing a rule of strict silence. The arrangement of the monks' quarters around a large walled cloister can be clearly seen. The central building within the grounds of the Priory was the Church, the tower being still intact. The ruins, open to the public, are maintained by English Heritage. Adjoining is the former Priory Guest House, still partly in use.

.... AND MODERN

Microwave radio station
on Beacon Hill

INGLEBY CROSS to BEACON HILL

At Ingleby Cross, go straight on, passing the Blue Bell Inn on the right. Cross over the new bypass and continue past Arncliffe Hall and Church and some farm buildings that have been converted into houses. When the road turns sharp right enter a field-gate on the left and go up the field to another gate at the top, there meeting a forest road. Waste no time searching for a path diagonally up the steep wooded slopes (as indicated on Ordnance 2½" maps) – new forest roads have cut it to shreds and undergrowth has made a direct way to the top of Beacon Hill impassable. There is now no practicable alternative to following the forest road to the right for a full mile to the forest boundary, where turn sharp left (a sign says 'Cleveland Way') on a rising track through woodland to the top of the moor above the trees. Now continue with a wall on the right, in heather and amongst regenerated birches, past a microwave radio station of revolting appearance, until arrival at the Ordnance Survey column (numbered S.4413) on the far side of the wall. (This column was originally the starting point of the Lyke Wake Walk. Now the walk starts at the Sheepwash Car Park half a mile further east.)

Notice especially the attractive Arncliffe Hall, a Georgian house designed by John Carr of York (1754)

Mount Grace Priory can be visited en route by a path from Park House — but if the day's sights are set beyond the B1257 road at Hasty Bank there isn't time for this detour: save the Priory for a separate visit in the future.

Osmotherley has a Youth Hostel; turn left when you reach a road.

The Ordnance column on Beacon Hill, looking north-east

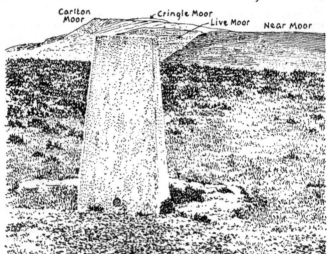

looking north-east across Scarth Nick.
The path to Scugdale is indicated (‒‒‒‒).

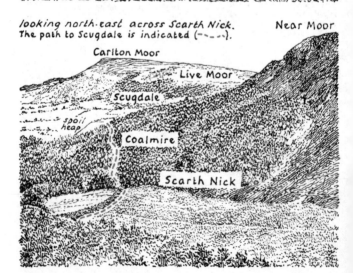

Beacon Hill

Beacon Hill, although less than a thousand feet above sea level, is a splendid viewpoint,* the panorama being greatly enhanced by its abrupt rise from the plains, the hill forming an upthrust cornerstone. Southwards, stretching apparently to the bounds of the earth, is the Vale of York; westwards is the long line of the Pennines beyond the Vale of Mowbray, a conspicuous indentation indicating Swaledale; northwards the hills of Durham are seen across the Cleveland Plain and Teesside — a wide prospect indeed, and, standing here, one can readily appreciate the importance of this signalling station long ago. It is to the east, however, that attention should be focussed, for in this direction is the line our march follows: the scene is a wilderness of heather moors sharply terminated by the pronounced Cleveland escarpment. It promises well.

※ In summer much of the view is now obscured by trees.

From the Ordnance column keep to the well-blazed path by the wall, north-east, as far as a gate (which is closely followed by another), from which it heads across the open moor as a wide scar in the heather, declining gently at first and then, when the wall again comes alongside, steeply to the tarmac road in Scarth Nick. Here turn left for a few yards and right at a cattle grid with a Cleveland Way signpost where a gateway admits to a woodland path that bends right and then left and joins a forest road. Near a pair of green seats on the left there commences a steep descent into the pleasant valley of Scugdale. When you come to a forest road turn left and then right onto a distinct path that bends right and continues up the valley.

Scugdale, from Coalmire

The path to
Live Moor is
indicated
(— — — —)

Carlton Moor

Live Moor

*Cairn on tumulus,
summit of Live Moor*

Carlton Moor

The path up Scugdale is as wide and well-defined as a gravel footway in an urban public park, and, being rural, is even more pleasant, the valley being wooded, with many fine deciduous trees alongside the beck and newer coniferous plantations on the higher slopes. After three-quarters of a mile the path becomes muddy, but the mud can be avoided by turning left through a kissing gate by a Cleveland Way signpost. The field thus entered slopes down to another gate giving access to a ford on a tributary of Scugdale Beck. Across this, a road is joined at a bridge over the main stream and followed up to a junction with the main valley-road. Here, to the right of a red pillar box, a path goes up the facing hillside, passing a disused iron mine (hidden from view by trees), then curving left and keeping below a plantation until a break in the latter is reached. Turning sharp right, ascend this break: it is steep but paved with stones. At the top is the open moor. There is no mistaking the path, which climbs very clearly onto the plateau of Live Moor, and is plainly visible beyond on the long slope of Carlton Moor. The route is now straightforward and foolproof, needing neither direction signs nor directions. Just keep plodding ahead.

The ford in Scugdale

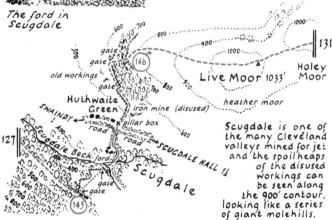

Scugdale is one of the many Cleveland valleys mined for jet and the spoil heaps of the disused workings can be seen along the 900' contour, looking like a series of giant molehills.

Boundary stone and Ordnance column,
summit of Carlton Moor

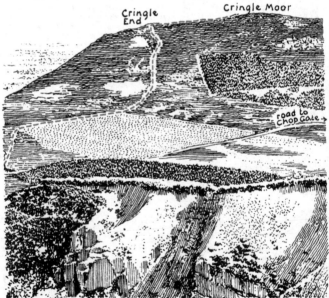

Cringle Moor, from the old alum workings on Carlton Moor.
The path to Cringle Moor is indicated (—·—·—).

Along the gentle rise to Carlton Moor is a line of inscribed boundary stones, one of them plumb in the middle of the broad path. As the top is breasted a great surprise awaits walkers who have not done their homework by reading up the route in advance. For half a mile the landscape is eerily lunar, the heather having been stripped off and the surface bulldozed and levelled to make runways for a gliding club whose buildings can be seen ahead. The path keeps to the left of the runway, following the edge of the rising escarpment to the Ordnance Survey column (No. S.4421) on the top of Carlton Moor; note below the conspicuous pink spoilheaps of the old jet workings strung along the hillside. This is a bold viewpoint with an uninterrupted prospect forward to the next height on the route, Cringle Moor; more to the north the sharp peak of Roseberry Topping (accentuated by quarrying into a miniature Matterhorn) is conspicuous and the monument to Captain Cook on Easby Moor can be distinguished. A motor road runs through the depression ahead (Carlton Bank); descend to it, roughly, along the edge of a crater (a disused alum mine) that has radically changed the natural contours of the ground. Cross the unmetalled road and the public road and continue to the flat moor beyond; then ascend, with a wall on the left, to the stony promontory of Cringle End, another fine viewpoint.

Carlton Moor was for centuries a place of work; more recently it has been a place of leisure. Gliding is a fine sport, a thrilling and graceful exercise, and it creates no noise or litter — but not even the most ardent enthusiast will claim that the landscape has been improved by its conversion to runways and some may even agree that a large tract of natural scenery has been despoiled. Well, there can be no comment from an 'off-comer', except to say that if such an operation was to be planned for the top of Helvellyn all hell would be let loose. (Note: In December 2008 the club announced that all flying activities had been suspended until further notice.)

Cringle End 135 · viewpoint · Carlton Lane · Carlton Bank · café · road · gate · felled · CHOP GATE 3½ · alum works (disused) · 148 · Carlton Moor -1338' · private road · old jet workings · hangars and clubhouse (Carlton Moor Gliding Club) · 147 · heather moor · 129 · Holey Moor

Boundary stone, view indicator and seat,
Cringle End

Cold Moor, from Cringle Moor

The path to Cold Moor
is indicated (~~~~~)

Cairn on tumulus,
summit of Cringle Moor

Hasty Bank, from Cold Moor
The path to Hasty Bank is indicated (·-·-·-·)

The summit of Cold Moor

Hasty Bank

looking back to Cold Moor (overtopped by Cringle Moor), from the top of the Wainstones.

The Wainstones:
the lower rocks

The Wainstones:
the upper rocks

looking across Clay Bank Top from Hasty Bank

The path to Urra Moor
is indicated (- - - -)

Clay Bank Top

car park

Cringle Moor is the finest elevation so far reached along the escarpment, being not only the second highest summit on the Cleveland Hills but having a steep and craggy declivity falling from its northern rim. The path turns up along the edge of the downfall, not visiting the actual summit of the moor, which is crowned with a tumulus and a cairn, and then goes down to a depression, with walled enclosures, beyond which it ascends to the top of Cold Moor, an airy dome carpeted with heather and bilberry. History then repeats itself, Cold Moor being descended to a similar depression with walled enclosures beyond which is another rise. But this one is different, being decorated with a cluster of fanged and pinnacled rocks, the Wainstones: a popular rock-climbing ground. Other groups of large boulders are nearby. There are natural shelters here from rain and wind (and sun!). This is an enjoyable section, a change from heather, and there is no difficulty in scrambling between the buttresses to the easy ground above. You will like the Wainstones.

Broughton Plantations   800
                         900
                         1000

Cringle
End
view indicator
and seat   KIRKBY (path)
131   150   151   137
                                            gap gap
                    1000   gate   gate   The
                                    Cold   Wainstones
tumulus *   Moor   Hasty
tumulus ▲ 1417'   1317'   Bank
Cringle   1300   1200 1100   1000
Moor   1200 1100 1000

heather moor

The view indicator
on Cringle End is a
memorial to Alec Falconer (1884-1968),
who, under the pseudonym of 'Rambler,'
was a champion of walkers' interests.

At Clay Bank Top.......

Clay Bank Top, where the road B1257 from Bilsdale crosses a natural (but artificially afforested) pass through the hills and starts its descent to the Cleveland Plain, is obviously a place for taking stock.

Most walkers on arrival here from Ingleby Cross will be feeling the effect of 12 up and down miles and be ready to call it a day. But where can a bed be found? There are no habitations near and they must be sought, but north or south? The nearest accommodation is at Maltkin House (tel. 01642 778216). Head south for half a mile and turn left, passing through the hamlet of Urra. Failing that there is Newlands House in Great Broughton (tel. 01642 712619), where transport is provided to and from Clay Bank Top.

Only strong walkers should consider proceeding further on the route today. Beyond the B1257 there is but one habitation before Glaisdale, and this is the Lion Inn at Blakey (tel. 01751 417320), where bed and breakfast is provided. There are also camping facilities if booked in advance. The Lion is 10 miles distant and it could be reached in 3 hours, the walking being remarkably easy.

SECTION MAP : CLAY BANK TOP to GLAISDALE : 18¾ miles

Detailed maps and narrative on pages 136 - 149

The Jurassic Escarpment

The ridge of high ground that runs to the west from Clay Bank Top over Hasty Bank, Cold Moor and Cringle Moor and which continues in the opposite direction to Urra Moor forms part of an escarpment of Jurassic limestone that extends all the way to Dorset. From Beacon Hill it heads south, forming the Hambleton and Howardian Hills. After that there is a gap; then the formation appears again as a narrow ridge running north and south from Lincoln. Then it gives rise to the hills of Northamptonshire and the Cotswolds and finally reaches the south coast near Bridport. Throughout its length the limestone is used in the construction of beautiful stone buildings. The highest point on the escarpment is Round Hill on Urra Moor, which is shown on the map above.

HASTY BANK to URRA MOOR

Hasty Bank is even better than Cringle Moor, the Wainstones being succeeded by a fine traverse along its edge and exciting glimpses down a fringe of steep crags; ahead, across a profound gap, is seen the next stage of the walk over Urra Moor. The path descends a steep slope, now beautifully engineered, with spoilheaps in view, to a kissing gate at the junction of a forest fence and a stone wall. Beyond this a flight of steps leads down to a tarmac road, the important B1257 linking Helmsley and Stokesley.

← Here consult the notes opposite.

The route crosses the road to a gate directly opposite: this is Hagg's Gate. Go through it and up by the wall serving as a forest boundary. The path is distinct on the ground here, being neatly paved with stone slabs. Above a gate in a fence it wriggles up to the left of a cleft in a rock outcrop to reach easier slopes above. Note the ancient dykes on the right, the original purpose of which is obscure. Also the stunted larches over the wall on the left, the last trees that will be seen at close quarters for the next 17 miles. The path goes on as straight as an arrow along the level peaty crest of Carr Ridge.

Hasty Bank is the most impressive of the Cleveland Hills and its fine summit deserves a distinctive name of its own, Hasty Bank properly being the southern slope of the hill above a farmhouse of that name. It deserves a cairn, too.

looking back from the firebreak on Urra Moor

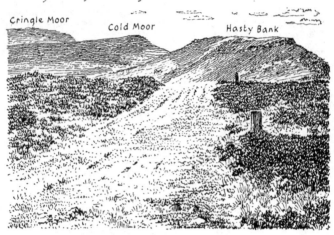

Cringle Moor Cold Moor Hasty Bank

cairn on tumulus, Urra Moor

Ordnance column on tumulus, summit of Urra Moor

The actual top is Round Hill (a reference to the tumulus), usually named Botton Head.

URRA MOOR to BLOWORTH

*The Hand Stone and the old road,
Urra Moor*

The path along Carr Ridge starts to rise gently to Urra Moor. The surroundings are featureless, but it is interesting to see, eastwards on the hillside across the hollow of Ingleby Botton, a distinct scar indicating the incline of the old Rosedale railway, with which we shall soon be on intimate terms. Before long the path bends slightly left and continues as wide as a road (which it originally was), passing a tumulus (cairned) on the right. An Ordnance column on the left (No. 2988), also on a tumulus, marks the highest point on the Cleveland Hills. On the 'roadside' nearby is the Hand Stone, bearing a carving of a hand on its south face, and, a little farther on, the Face Stone, with a carving of a face. Other inscribed stones are met as the highway descends gradually to the old railway.

The Rosedale Ironstone Railway

The Rosedale Branch was constructed in 1861, when the North Eastern Railway extended its lines in Cleveland by incorporating a mineral line, replacing it by a single standard-gauge track and continuing it by means of a mile-long incline across the high moors at an elevation of around 1300' for ten miles to the ironstone mines in Rosedale — a considerable engineering achievement, the contours being so closely followed that, throughout a long passage across several watersheds, cuttings, embankments and levelling sufficed to carry the line around the heads of intervening valleys without the use of any bridges or tunnels. The track was unenclosed by fences and had no signalling equipment, operation being controlled by staff based on Blakey Ridge. This remarkable enterprise was undertaken to convey the high-grade iron ore mined on the Rosedale hillsides, which had in fact been worked from a very early date, possibly for two thousand years, as evidenced by ancient furnaces, and was enjoying a booming prosperity in the mid nineteenth century. Road transport via Pickering was inadequate to cope with the output; the construction of a high-level railway over the moors, linking with other lines that served the big blast furnaces of Teesside and Durham, was a bold venture, and, despite storms and blizzards, appears to have well succeeded, upwards of ten million tons of iron ore being conveyed along it. Only freight trains used the line but occasionally a few passengers were carried.

The railway as originally laid entered Rosedale by way of Blakey Ridge and terminated at the Bank Top mines on the west side of the valley, where the main workings were located and where relics are still to be seen. In 1865 it was extended by a branch running around the head of the valley to mines on the eastern flank from the staff control point at Blakey, which then became a junction.

By the turn of the century ironstone production was in decline and the railway less in demand, and finally it was closed and dismantled in 1929. The line was lonely and isolated, and threatened by extreme weather conditions, but the regular passage of freight trains brought a pulse of life to the wilderness through which they passed. Today the track is still there, but it is silent; yet even in death it has lost nothing of its grace and dignity but remains a mute and inspiring monument to the men who planned and built it over a century ago, a permanent way that will remain permanent, a reminder of an achievement that deserves to be, and will be, long remembered.

A map of the railway is given overleaf ——→

A fascinating booklet called ROSEDALE MINES AND RAILWAY by R. H. Hayes and J. G. Rutter (£3.50) is obtainable locally or from the Ryedale Folk Museum, Hutton le Hole, near Pickering.

BLOWORTH to DALE HEAD, FARNDALE

Bloworth Crossing

When the road bends left at a post take the path straight on, cutting the corner off to join the railway track; bear right along the cinders of the permanent way. Two gates across it are passed; at the second the track is crossed by a rough moorland road. This is Bloworth Crossing; at this point there is a glimpse of Bransdale to the south. The Cleveland Way now turns off to the north and will not be met again until it is rejoined on the sea-cliffs at Hawsker Bottoms. Keep on along the railway track, responding to the easy walking by a noticeable increase in speed. Beyond a cutting Farndale is in view and the track loops around the head of this valley on an even contour, keeping slightly below the watershed. No question of short-cutting the loops arises: one look at the terrain flanking the permanent way is enough to rule it out as a possibility. With little of interest to see, you might as well be improving your knowledge by reading the story of the railway as you go along. Don't worry, you won't fall into any holes.

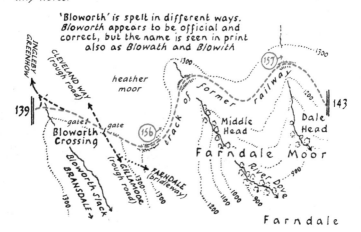

'Bloworth' is spelt in different ways. Bloworth appears to be official and correct, but the name is seen in print also as Blowath and Blowith

The Rosedale Ironstone Railway
MAP

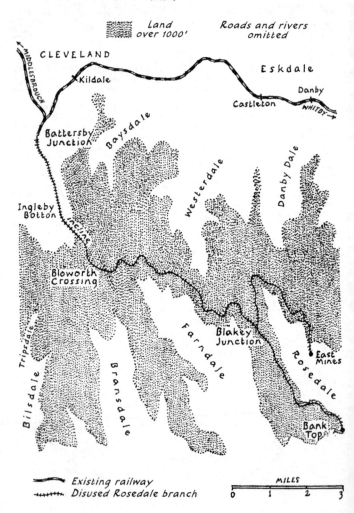

Land over 1000'

Roads and rivers omitted

Existing railway
Disused Rosedale branch

MILES
0 1 2 3

DALE HEAD, FARNDALE to HIGH BLAKEY MOOR

The long embankment near Esklets

Fast walking continues along the railway track and speeds will now have accelerated to 5 m.p.h. Here the route takes us through the largest area of heather moorland in England. In the year 2000 170 square miles (nearly a third of the National Park) became a Site of Special Scientific Interest. The moors came into existence about 2500 years ago and have been managed for grouse shooting since the 1850s. They are noted for golden plovers and merlins.

Resist the attractions of lovely Farndale (which is noted for its daffodils) and surge on happily along the permanent way. We're enjoying this: it's like playing at trains again. Better than that, it's like being a train yourself.

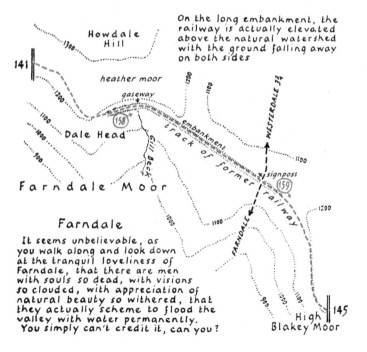

On the long embankment, the railway is actually elevated above the natural watershed with the ground falling away on both sides

Howdale Hill

1300

141

heather moor

gateway

1200

158

Dale Head

embankment

track of former railway

WESTERDALE 73

signpost

159

1100

1200

Farndale Moor

Farndale

FARNDALE

1100

1000

Farndale

It seems unbelievable, as you walk along and look down at the tranquil loveliness of Farndale, that there are men with souls so dead, with visions so clouded, with appreciation of natural beauty so withered, that they actually scheme to flood the valley with water permanently. You simply can't credit it, can you?

High Blakey Moor

145

A good moment. At a curve in the last railway cutting the Lion Inn comes into view on the skyline ahead.

The Lion Inn is the most obvious halting-place on the whole route: the first habitation since Huthwaite, 16 miles back. Rooms are let on a bed-and-breakfast basis and food is served all day. Camping is permitted if arranged in advance. (Across the road is High Blakey House, where accommodation is also available.) If starting from Clay Bank Top, arranging a room for the night is of less importance, the miles continuing very easy to Glaisdale.

Buses currently run to Castleton and Pickering in the summer, the last ones leaving at 5.30 p.m.

The Lion Inn, Blakey

Dating from 1553, the Lion is an isolated moorland inn. Situated amongst decayed relics of industry, it once catered for ironworkers and coalminers but today it serves walkers and motorists (and looks somewhat different from this drawing).

Blakey Howe

Behind the inn is Blakey Howe, a *tumulus* excavated to provide a sheltered and secluded hollow for cockfighting, hence its alternative name of Cockpit Hill.

HIGH BLAKEY MOOR to DANBY HIGH MOOR

When the railway starts its great loop around the head of Blakey Gill, a solitary building appears on the skyline ahead. Mark it well. It is the Lion Inn, an important landmark and the next objective. As the track curves round it vanishes from sight, but a 'Lyke Wake Walk' arrow indicates a path thereto. Use this, and say farewell to the old Rosedale railway. And thanks. It has been a great help. The rails have been taken up but it still serves mankind.

← Here consult the notes opposite

The east branch of the railway runs around the head of Rosedale and could be used for a further mile from the fields east of the Lion Inn, but this is not recommended. Instead go north along the road (it is quiet, with wide, easy verges) for a mile to a distinctive stone boundary post known as Old Margery (there isn't a young one around). Opposite, a grooved path can be used to cut a big bend in the road but becomes indistinct and is not a time-saver.

WESTERDALE 2

CASTLETON

Danby High Moor

1300 road 1300

tumuli

Ralph Crosses

road

White Cross (Fat Betty)

Monument

163   147

Rosedale Head

old pits

heather moor

1400

boundary stone (Margery Bradley)

1200

track of former railway

River Seven

1100

1000

162   road   1100   1200   1000

track of former railway

heather moor

1300

1300

161

tumulus (Blakey Howe)

Rosedale

143

160

track of former railway

1200   1100   1000

Blakey Gill

00

'Lyke Wake Walk' stone

Lion Inn Blakey

road

BLAKEY JUNCTION

BLAKEY JUNCTION

HUTTON LE HOLE 6½

High Blakey Moor

Monuments
at Rosedale Head

top left:
  Ralph Cross
    (Young Ralph)

top middle:
  White Cross
    (Fat Betty)

top right:
  Ralph Cross
    (Old Ralph)

Frank Elgee Memorial

A curve in the Rosedale road can be by-passed by following
a series of boundary stones, and the corner of the Fryup
road may also be by-passed, but both short-cuts are often
revoltingly slimy and it is then better to keep to the tarmac.
At the Fryup turn (signpost:'single track road') the Lyke Wake
Walk is departed from and not met again.   The road to
Fryup gives excellent walking and views of Eskdale with the
sharp peak of Roseberry Topping conspicuous ten miles
northwest, but after half a mile is forsaken in favour of a
branch to the right leading to the solitary building now in sight.
This is Trough House, a shooting box.   At one time it provided
shelter, like the one to the south of Nine Standards, but now it
is kept locked. Notice the Ordnance Survey benchmark on the
side of the hut facing the path.   Beyond here the track
deteriorates, the gravel giving way to mud and ruts, although
its course is plain to see rounding the head of Great Fryup Dale
– of which there is a full-length view – and is accompanied by
a clear path, which after ascending slightly finally heads
straight for Glaisdale and joins a tarmac road. The ground now
forms a ridge between Great Fryup Dale (left) and Glaisdale
Head (right) and the road runs along its crest. Follow it north.

Danby High Moor is typical of this wedge of high country: now uninhabited and inhospitable but yielding evidence by the excavation of its many barrows or burial mounds of a primitive people who lived here three or four thousand years ago.

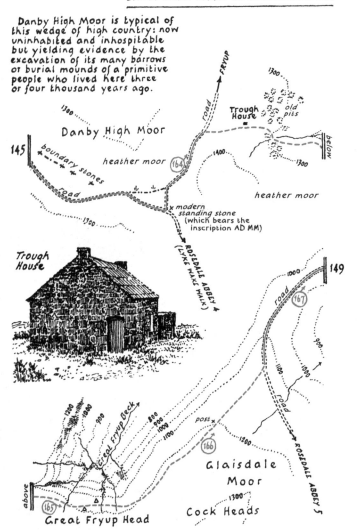

Danby High Moor

1300

boundary stones

145

heather moor

164

road

1300

x modern standing stone (which bears the inscription AD MM)

(LYKE WAKE WALK)

ROSEDALE ABBEY 4

road FRYUP

Trough House

old pits

1300

below

1300

1400

heather moor

Trough House

149

1000

road

167

900

1000

1100

Great Fryup Beck

1200

1100

1000

900

800

900

1000

1100

post x

1200

166

Glaisdale Moor

road

ROSEDALE ABBEY 5

above

165

Great Fryup Head

1300

Cock Heads

Beggar's Bridge

After passing a fine cairn, 100 yards away on the right, the road turns slightly left just before an Ordnance Survey column. Leave it at this point and take the cart-track going straight ahead: a sign declares this to be unsuitable for motors, but for foot-travellers it is a way par excellence heading directly down the declining ridge (Glaisdale Rigg), towards the end of which, with a wall close ahead, the track bears to the left (ignore all others) and descends alongside a fence, acquiring a tarmac surface beyond a gate and passing Glaisdale Hall Farm to reach civilisation in the form of a modern housing estate at the top end of the village of Glaisdale. Turn right, and if in search of lodging or refreshment go down by the long terrace, where sundry delicacies including raw sausages may be acquired in exchange for money and where there are possibilities of obtaining accommodation. The route follows the road round to the railway station and the River Esk. The scenery in the vicinity of the river is charming. Pass under the railway bridge to take a photograph of the early 17th century Beggar's Bridge, as everyone does, then return under the railway and immediately take the path, steep initially, over a footbridge into East Arncliffe Wood. The path is easy to follow, but muddy in places, much of it being roughly paved with stone slabs.

ENVIRONS OF BEGGAR'S BRIDGE

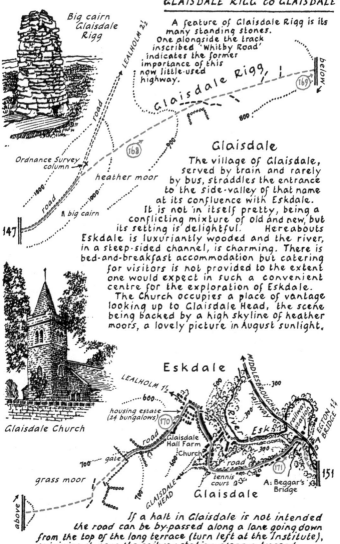

Big cairn Glaisdale Rigg

LEALHOLM 2½

A feature of Glaisdale Rigg is its many standing stones. One alongside the track inscribed 'Whitby Road' indicates the former importance of this now little-used highway.

Glaisdale Rigg

169

below

800

Ordnance Survey column

163

900

Glaisdale

heather moor

road

800

900

A big cairn

147

Glaisdale

The village of Glaisdale, served by train and rarely by bus, straddles the entrance to the side-valley of that name at its confluence with Eskdale.
It is not in itself pretty, being a conflicting mixture of old and new, but its setting is delightful.   Hereabouts Eskdale is luxuriantly wooded and the river, in a steep-sided channel, is charming. There is bed-and-breakfast accommodation but catering for visitors is not provided to the extent one would expect in such a convenient centre for the exploration of Eskdale.
The Church occupies a place of vantage looking up to Glaisdale Head, the scene being backed by a high skyline of heather moors, a lovely picture in August sunlight.

Eskdale

MIDDLESBROUGH RAILWAY

LEALHOLM 1½

300

600

housing estate (24 bungalows)

170

River

railway station

EGTON BRIDGE 1½

road

Glaisdale Hall Farm

Church

Esk

300

171

151

Glaisdale Church

700

gate

road

tennis court

A: Beggar's Bridge

grass moor

700

GLAISDALE HEAD

Glaisdale

above

If a halt in Glaisdale is not intended the road can be by-passed along a lane going down from the top of the long terrace (turn left at the Institute), rejoining it near the railway station along a by-road.

SECTION MAP : *GLAISDALE to ROBIN HOOD'S BAY* : 19 miles

Detailed maps
and narrative
on pages 150·163

This final stage of the walk has a wide variety of scene:
a lovely river and woodlands, heather moors, charming
villages, prehistoric relics, a stately waterfall, a forest
trail, steam locomotives, and, to end it, an exhilarating
cliff path and the North Sea extending to a far horizon,
all different subjects alike only in distinctive appeal. In
fact many walkers will consider this section the best of
all, quite apart from the satisfaction of accomplishing a
mission. The 'going' for the greater part of it is easy and
a strong walker could reach Robin Hood's Bay from Glaisdale
before nightfall, but country like this is much too good to
be hurried over, much too interesting to be appreciated in
full measure if limbs are tired, and it is suggested that the
day's activity be halted at Hawsker (the first opportunity
of a bed after Littlebeck), leaving the last few miles to the
Bay — a splendid finish along the cliffs — until next day.
    It will be noticed that, towards the end of the journey, the
shortest route to the Bay is not taken, five miles being added
by a wide detour to the north around Hawsker.   This detour
can, of course, be omitted and the Bay reached more directly
by road, in which event an overnight stay en route will not
normally be necessary.   The reason for the detour is simply
to give a fitting culmination to the walk, a counterpart to
the start over St. Bees Head, reaching Robin Hood's Bay over
the top of the sea-cliffs, by far the finest approach.   It is
a little odd that this *west-to-east* walk started *north-west*
and ends *south-west*, but that's the way the best land lies.
    You will really enjoy this last section to the Bay, whatever
the condition of your blisters, so much that you will regret
leaving behind each of its many attractive features.   And
when the North Sea comes into full view and you recall your
last sighting of the Irish Sea you will be glad you didn't stay
on in Patterdale. Lakeland is all very well but by resisting
its lure you have seen so much new and interesting and lovely
country that, on reflection, you wouldn't have missed for worlds.
Come on now, admit it.

Egton Bridge

Egton is a village on the hillside a mile north of the Esk. The more sequestered Egton Bridge is the part of the parish built on the river banks and served by the railway. Here, as everywhere in the middle reaches of Eskdale, the scenery is delightful, a wealth of trees bordering the river and a belt of rich pastures, broken by extensive woodlands, descending to the valley from a surround of wild moors. The stone bridge – built in 1993 – looks just like the 1758 original (unlike the previous iron bridge, which was quite out of character). There are some houses of distinction and two hotels of attractive design, but the building most worth a visit is the Roman Catholic church, which has coloured bas-reliefs panels on its exterior walls and ornate decoration internally on the ribbed roof. In such a sylvan setting little awareness is felt of the enclosing moors, desolate and inhospitable but revealing much of archaeological interest, mainly of prehistoric origin but with evidences of the Roman occupation of the area.

R.C. Church,
Egton Bridge

The path through East Arncliffe Wood emerges on a quiet tarmac road (the moor road to Rosedale). Go down this to the left and so reach Egton Bridge, in lovely wooded surroundings. Just past the Horseshoe Hotel turn left along a delightful path that crosses two branches of the River Esk by well-designed stepping stones. (If the stepping stones are under water, use the bridge.) When you come to a road turn right, then left in 200 yards and then right at a 'Coast to Coast' signpost onto the Egton estate road.

Eskdale

EGTON

300

railway station

200

GLAISDALE (road)

R.C. Church

113

railway

300
200
2

Egton Manor

Egton Bridge

private road

153

19

River Esk

road

KEY GREEN

River Esk

200

East Arncliffe Wood

112

road

300

ROSEDALE ABBEY 7

'Arncliff' is the Ordnance spelling; locally, 'Arncliff' or 'Arncliffe' is preferred.

Grosmont

At Grosmont a traveller down the valley of the Esk first becomes aware, albeit slightly, of urban influences. Here are the steep declivities to the river, the rich woodlands that so characterise the higher reaches, but the railway station (a junction of lines), the debris of iron workings, and a faint air of commercialism suggest that the best of the scenery is being left behind. Nevertheless it is an excellent centre for touring the district : there are shops and some accommodation is provided. A priory existed here at one time ; today the religious needs of the Anglican community are served by a church set back from the houses in a hanging garden of trees by the river. Road access to the village is very steep on all sides, which would appear to explain the absence of a bus service: the railway here, a scenic joy, is still important.

The North Yorkshire Moors Railway

Steam locomotives standing in Grosmont Station

The railway from Whitby to Pickering, leaving the Eskdale line at Grosmont, threaded a tortuous course through scenery of rare beauty, and popular opinion considered it one of the finest railways in the country. It was one of George Stephenson's early creations. Alas, like so many others, its day is done and a notable engineering achievement would have become yet another historical relic but for the valiant efforts of a band of enthusiasts, the North Yorkshire Moors Historical Railway Trust, to preserve and continue to operate privately the section from Grosmont to Pickering with steam locomotives and rolling stock they have acquired. George Stephenson would approve.

Bridge over the Esk at Grosmont

The estate road passes a farm and then the former Toll Bar, which although no longer functional as such still displays details of the tolls formerly charged, these being made for the passage both of the living and the dead (Hearse...6d), before emerging on the Egton-Grosmont road, which follow to the right over a bridge (this is farewell to the River Esk) and past playing fields to the village of Grosmont, where reprieved steam locomotives may be seen at the Viewing Gallery. Go over the level crossing and up the steep road beyond (1 in 3), ignoring two branches to Whitby on the left. As height is gained a fine retrospective view of Eskdale opens up.

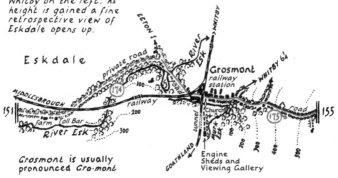

Eskdale

151   155

Grosmont is usually pronounced Gro·mont

Low Bride Stones

High Bride Stones

The Old Mill, Littlebeck

After stepping gingerly across a cattle grid the open moor is reached. On the right are the Low Bride Stones (not worth looking for) and the more impressive High Bride Stones, some standing, some fallen, which are well seen from the road. When a double gate is reached the sea comes into view. Turn left along a path leading to the busy Whitby—Pickering road. Now Whitby and its Abbey can be seen on the left. Turn left for a quarter of a mile and then right opposite a sign saying 'Blue Bank ½ mile ahead' onto a rough track. This crosses open ground, enters a lane and is joined by a road from Sleights for the steep descent to the hamlet of Littlebeck, a miniature Arcadia embowered in trees, a glimpse of heaven for nerve-frayed town-dwellers. Across the beck and round the corner, near a seat on the right, is the signposted start of the path to Falling Foss. Use this: it is easy to follow, but a branch to the right early on, in an area of old spoil heaps, is misleading. Thereafter the way is clear up the valley, always amongst trees, and finally rising gently to a massive boulder out of which, amazingly, has been carved a splendid shelter with seats: in beautiful lettering the name 'The Hermitage', the year 1790 and the initials G.C. are inscribed in the stone. Here take the upper of two paths, rising towards the farm buildings of Newton House.

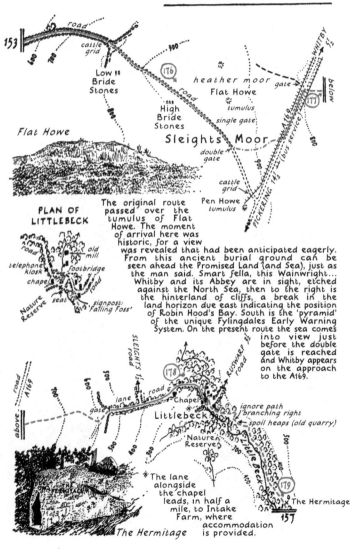

PLAN OF LITTLEBECK

The original route passed over the tumulus of Flat Howe. The moment of arrival here was historic, for a view that had been anticipated eagerly. From this ancient burial ground can be seen ahead the Promised Land (and Sea), just as the man said. Smart fella, this Wainwright... Whitby and its Abbey are in sight, etched against the North Sea, then to the right is the hinterland of cliffs, a break in the land horizon due east indicating the position of Robin Hood's Bay. South is the 'pyramid' of the unique Fylingdales Early Warning System. On the present route the sea comes into view just before the double gate is reached and Whitby appears on the approach to the A169.

* The lane alongside the chapel leads, in half a mile, to Intake Farm, where accommodation is provided.

The Hermitage

157

Falling Foss

THE HERMITAGE to GRAYSTONE HILLS

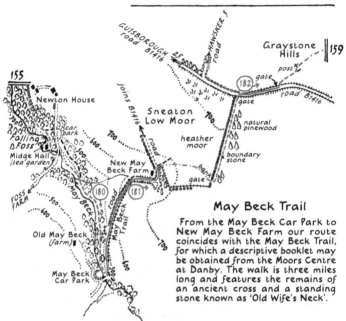

May Beck Trail

From the May Beck Car Park to New May Beck Farm our route coincides with the May Beck Trail, for which a descriptive booklet may be obtained from the Moors Centre at Danby. The walk is three miles long and features the remains of an ancient cross and a standing stone known as 'Old Wife's Neck'.

Without entering the grounds of Newton House, continue along a level path outside the estate wall, soon descending slightly to Falling Foss in surroundings of bewitching beauty. The waterfall is best seen in winter when there are no leaves on the trees. Pass in front of Midge Hall, now the Falling Foss Tea Garden, cross the wooden footbridge (where there is a notice entitled 'Rules for playing Poohsticks') and walk upstream 70 yards to a stone bridge. The route originally went straight on here and crossed May Beck by stepping stones, but now the stepping stones have gone and it is necessary to turn left over a second bridge and then right alongside the stream, where a boardwalk has been provided. Continue alongside the stream to the May Beck Car Park. Go up the road, which overlooks the wooded valley just traversed, but beyond New May Beck Farm strike across the heather moor on the right to reach a gate in a wall. Turn left and follow the wall to the busy B1416 road. The quickest way to Hawsker is to turn left then take the unsignposted road to the right, but lovers of heather moors with time to spare should turn right along the wide verges of the road and escape from it at a gate on the left.

A hundred yards after leaving the road the path divides into two.   Take the left branch, which leads to a post inscribed with the words 'Coast to Coast'. Further posts show the way to go, but they can be difficult to see, and it is easy to go astray.   300 yards away on the right is an old stone cross, which is visible from the path for some distance on the skyline but may not be noticed. In half a mile, by a short post, a path on the right leads to the main Scarborough–Whitby road (A171). Here a signpost gives the thrilling news that Robin Hood's Bay is only two miles distant along the facing side-road, and if it is wished to save time by avoiding the big detour to Hawsker you could be there, licking ice-cream and eyeing the girls, in half an hour, mission accomplished....   But faithful followers of the recommended route will turn their faces to the moor again and apply themselves to more trudging through the heather, now heading north.   When a tumulus ahead makes a slight rise in the skyline keep left of it to a gate in a fence, and go down rough ground to another gate giving access to a muddy lane that leads to a corner on a tarmac road. Here bear right for Hawsker, crossing the main road to the village street.   Enough has now been done for the day and accommodation can be sought, but those who now really have the bit between their teeth and two hours of daylight left can push on along the road signposted to Robin Hood's Bay (2½ miles), keeping ahead when it curves to the right and following a lane past a caravan site and then crossing the track of the former railway.   This latter, incidentally, gives a good fast walk to the Bay but like the tarmac road thereto is a temptation to be resisted.   Such reluctance to take the quickest ways to the Bay is rather suggestive of a cat playing with a mouse before administering the coup de grâce, but the fact is that the royal road to the Bay undoubtedly is the coast path, pouncing on the prey from the top of the cliffs. That's the way we'll go, so carry on down the lane and don't argue.

Hawsker
(omitting the TV aerials but including the drainpipes)

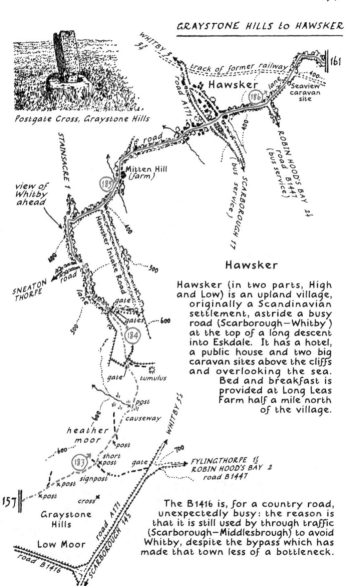

Postgate Cross, Graystone Hills

WHITBY 3¼

track of former railway

road A171

Hawsker

WHITBY 3

lane

Seaview caravan site

161

ROBIN HOOD'S BAY B1447 (bus service)

road

STAINSACRE 1

Mitten Hill (farm)

view of Whitby ahead

Hawsker Intake Road

SCARBOROUGH 1¾ (bus service)

SNEATON THORPE

road

lane

gate

gates

tumulus

gate

post

causeway

heather moor

post

short post

signpost

gate

WHITBY 5½

FYLINGTHORPE 1¼
ROBIN HOOD'S BAY 2
road B1447

157

post

post

cross

Graystone Hills

Low Moor

road A171

SCARBOROUGH 14½

road B1416

Hawsker

Hawsker (in two parts, High and Low) is an upland village, originally a Scandinavian settlement, astride a busy road (Scarborough—Whitby) at the top of a long descent into Eskdale. It has a hotel, a public house and two big caravan sites above the cliffs and overlooking the sea. Bed and breakfast is provided at Long Leas Farm half a mile north of the village.

The B1416 is, for a country road, unexpectedly busy: the reason is that it is still used by through traffic (Scarborough—Middlesbrough) to avoid Whitby, despite the bypass which has made that town less of a bottleneck.

Maw Wyke Hole

Enter Northcliffe caravan site and go down its right-hand road. When the road bends right cut across to a post marking the start of a path with Oakham Beck on the left and water in great quantity palpably near ahead. The Coast Path is met at a signpost overlooking Maw Wyke Hole. After a halt to savour the acute personal satisfaction of arrival at the edge of the North Sea follow the Coast Path to the right. There is no difficulty of route finding, the path being in popular use and part of the long-distance Cleveland Way. Accompanying it most of the way is a wire fence, usually to landward. The cliff scenery is excellent. A first sighting of Robin Hood's Bay is eagerly awaited but delayed until Ness Point is finally rounded ...... but then, suddenly, there it is. Now for the coup de grâce!

Robin Hood's Bay

NORTH SEA
at last

WHITBY 4

Maw Wyke
Hole

signpost

Oakham Beck

187

ignore stile on right (signposted
'National Trust Centenary Path')

Northcliffe
caravan site

159

Hawsker
Bottoms

300

Railway Path (National Cycle Network Route 1)

400

highest
point

188

300

200

Coastguard
Station

Ness
Point

400

189

gate

gate

gate

high water mark

low water mark

reefs

300

WHITBY 5½
HAWSKER 2
road B1447

200

car
park

bus stand

FYLINGTHORPE ½
SCARBOROUGH 17
road B1447

100

Kings Beck

car
park

Robin Hood's Bay

promenade
'The Quarterdeck'

190

Well, that's it!!

Here the
path follows
what is known
as the Dinosaur
Coast. Eventually
civilisation is reached
in the form of an avenue of
modern villas, which could be
Suburbia anywhere, especially
with a name like Mount Pleasant
North. The real Robin Hood's Bay
is found by turning left down
the hill past the lower car park.
A narrow street with flights of steps
for pedestrians now descends very
steeply into a picturesque huddle
of red-roofed buildings literally
perched on the edge of the sea.
Proceed with
decorum to
the bottom of
the hill, to the
limit of terra firma,
where the tarmac ends
at a shingly beach
and the sea. Go
forward and put
your boot in the
first salt-water
puddle. By
this ritual
you will have
completed a
walk from one side of
England to the other.

Robin Hood's Bay

Robin Hood's Bay, locally known as Bay Town or simply as The Bay, was an obscure fishing village and reputedly a haunt of smugglers until its unique situation, medieval atmosphere and picturesque appearance began to earn for it a secondary livelihood from visitors. Today it is a showplace for tourists, an itinerary 'must', but happily its quaint features have been preserved. The coast here, ribbed with sandstone reefs and rich in fossils, is geologically interesting, but it is the 'town', the amazing cluster of red-roofed buildings perched one above another, the labyrinth of passageways and steps, crowded into a breach in the cliffs with remarkable economy of space, a nest crammed tight, that attracts most attention. Happily too private car traffic is halted at the top of the hill leading down to the shore: the narrow streets and alleys are pedestrian precincts. There are several shops and ample hotel and private cottage accommodation; with a Youth Hostel nearby. The railway has ceased to function but there are bus services to Whitby and Scarborough from the suburbia that has sprung up around the hinterland of the Bay.

Bay Town

The end of the road

Now you can rest on your laurels in the Bay Hotel with a pint, but (let there be no misunderstanding about this) you do so at your own expense. It's no use saying "charge it to Wainwright" as you could in days gone by at the Border Hotel, Kirk Yetholm. No, sonny, that game won't work here. Pay for your own. I'm skint.

INDEX TO PLACE-NAMES ON THE MAPS

This index lists only the place-names on the detailed route maps. Other references to these names, where they occur in the illustrations and notes accompanying the maps, will be found on the same or opposite page.

INDEX continued

INDEX continued

INDEX continued

INDEX continued

*There is one inadvertent
omission from the index
but this of no importance,
it being extremely unlikely
that any reader will wish
to refer to GREAT TONGUE
on page 31.*

*Some Personal notes
in conclusion*

I am beginning to have second thoughts about "official" long-distance footpaths. I am now not at all sure that they are wholly to be commended. Insofar as they get people into the fresh air, well and good, for urban existence today demands an occasional change of environment; insofar as they provide a challenge, well and good, for a life without challenges is tedious. But the wide publicity given to them brings disadvantages. The official blessing and opening of a long-distance path is headline news. The word goes forth and the world pulls on his boots.

The first of them, the Pennine Way, has already been so much used that it is fast losing its original appeal as a wilderness walk and becoming a too-popular parade. There are blazed tracks and litter where once there were neither. Some paths are so badly eroded that diversions have been necessary. Farmers along the route, faced with broken walls and straying stock, are being sorely tried. Sheep are crippling and choking themselves with broken glass and plastic bags. In time you won't need a map: just follow the trail of empty cans and orange peel.

Most walkers still walk for walking's sake, because they like doing it; not as an opportunity for mischief. These are the goodies, the folk who really enjoy an escape to the quietness of the countryside and the hills, leave no traces of their passage and cause no trouble. But there are also the baddies, attracted by the publicity given to official footpaths but careless about the country code, inconsiderate of others, rebels against conventions and customs and decent behaviour and a general nuisance. These are the inexperienced, who cannot read a map, and the complete nogs who have never seen one. Official footpaths are menaced by such. The trouble is that officially prescribed routes cannot be selective of their users. They are open to all. They invite all. They are used by all.

You don't need to have an official route to get you out into the open air. You don't have to wait for the Countryside Commission to say 'O.K. you can go!' You don't have to follow the crowds. In this country there are thousands of long-distance routes for walkers that have never suffered an official blessing (and are all the better for that) and any walker with initiative can plan his own itineraries simply by linking the public rights of way recorded on current issues of the 1" Ordnance maps. There is positively no end to the routes that can be worked out. You may follow high-level tracks over the hills; or circuit mountain watersheds; or march the boundary of your county, or any other; or trace old drove roads; or go from point A to point B, whether A and B are castles, Roman camps, stone circles, or whatever; or visit your maiden aunt in Bognor; or cross the country on canal towpaths; or follow rivers from source to sea.

And all on foot, using rights of way, causing no trespass and needing no permissions. The map of England is an oyster very rich in pearls. Plan your own marathon and do something never done before, something you will enjoy, a route that will take you to places often read about but never yet seen. You will be on your own, unhampered by human beings en bloc, relying on your own resources to complete what you set out to do. Preferably go alone and do it off your own bat, for it is the solitary walker, always, who most closely identifies himself with his surroundings, who observes as he goes along, who really feels the satisfaction of achievement. If you must have a friend choose one who is quiet.

This is the sort of thing I set out to do in this book. In offering the idea of a coast to coast walk I am not contradicting myself at all — there is nothing official about it: it is an example of what might be done without any opening speeches and fanfares : a personal venture. I describe the route I planned and walked, and, for any who care to tread in my footsteps, directions are given — it's a good expedition although I say it myself : ideal for connoisseurs of fine scenery — but I would feel I had succeeded better in arousing interest for the planning of private long-distance walks if the book induced some readers to follow instead their own star and find their own rainbow's end.

In planning the walk I had four main objectives:

1: to avoid towns;
2: to link together three National Parks;
3: to keep to high ground wherever practicable;
4: to use only rights of way and areas of open access.

The first was easy, Richmond being the only town visited and that by design; the second ensured a high quality of scenery throughout; the third, a personal preference, was practicable except for the crossing of the Vale of Mowbray; the fourth I hope I observed everywhere.

It took me a year and it was a journey of delight. St. Bees Head, habitat of countless seabirds, was a splendid start; Lakeland as ever was a sweet foretaste of heaven; the Westmorland plateau was a joy to walk upon, as limestone always is; the Pennine crossing was wilderness tramping, grim yet relieved by the larks and curlews and ill-fated grouse; the old lead mines of Swaledale, ugly yet fascinating; the Vale of Mowbray, tranquillity profound; the grand heather moors of Cleveland and finally quaint Robin Hood's Bay, with the north sea stretching into infinity. You could not have a better-defined start and finish, each with the waves lapping your boots, and the inbetween was (with reservations about the Vale of Mowbray) an inspiring pageant of beauty and interest. I can say now that I have walked from one coast of England to the other. A year ago I couldn't have said this.

It is a walk I recommend, not necessarily to undertake in a single journey, but in parts as place, time and weather become convenient. But as I said before, vary it to suit yourself: you may for example prefer a more exciting traverse of Lakeland; or feel that Tan Hill would please you more than Keld (incidentally, it wouldn't) or, in a magnificent finale, take to the Lyke Wake Walk instead of the easier route I followed myself. But always keep to rights of way and, of course, travel every inch of the way on foot. Then, with me, you will be able to say you have walked across England.

A comparison with the Pennine Way is inevitable. The Pennine Way is far longer and a greater challenge to stamina, but most of it lies over dreary moorlands. The Coast to Coast Walk is, in my opinion, immeasurably superior in scenic qualities, although it has no Hadrian's Wall to stimulate the imagination. You enjoy the Pennine Way, if at all, because it satisfies an ambition and is a personal achievement; certainly not for its ravishing scenery. The Coast to Coast Walk is enjoyable for its beauty, for the dramatic variations of landscape and for its many interesting relics, some rooted in prehistory. The start and finish of the Pennine Way are arbitrary, those of the Coast to Coast Walk are exact. One has a certain grandeur, the other a succession of charms. The Pennine Way is masculine; the Coast to Coast Walk has feminine characteristics. If there happens to be something in your temperament that makes you like the ladies the odds are that you will prefer the C. to C. You may not meet any, but you will be reminded of them. On the PW you never give them a thought .... well, hardly ever.

I finished the Pennine Way with relief, the Coast to Coast Walk with regret. That's the difference.

aw

June 1972

Reader's LOG OF THE JOURNEY

The remaining pages in this book are intended for the personal use of readers engaged on the walk.

The Log lists the various sections of the route, each providing a good day's walk and ending at a place where refreshment and accommodation are normally available.   Each section is subdivided into convenient parts for the use of those who cannot, or prefer not to, attempt the whole journey at one time; and for others who, because of disability, old age or infirmity, can only be 'half-day' or 'hour or two' walkers. For those who are 'supported' and victualled by friends with a car, intermediate points in each section where a car may wait are indicated

A walker doing the full journey at one go will be interested in the subdivisions only for the purpose of halting to record times of arrival and departure.

The following symbols are used in the Log:

√ : *point accessible by car*

X : *bus service*

N.G.R. : *National Grid Reference*

Miles { S : *in section*
{ C : *cumulative*

Times { A : *of arrival*
{ D : *of departure*

Better fill this in before you start

THIS BOOK BELONGS TO

Name:

Address:

If found unattended and obviously lost *please* send it to the above address.

LOG OF THE JOURNEY

Date	Section	N.G.R.	Miles S	Miles C	Times A	Times D	Weather
	X St. Bees (sea wall)	NX 960118	-	-			
	√ Sandwith	NX 964148	$4\frac{3}{4}$	$4\frac{3}{4}$			
	X Cleator	NY 015135	$8\frac{3}{4}$	$8\frac{3}{4}$			
	Dent	NY 038130	$10\frac{3}{4}$	$10\frac{3}{4}$			
	√ Kinniside Stone Circle	NY 060140	$12\frac{3}{4}$	$12\frac{3}{4}$			
	√ Ennerdale Bridge	NY 069159	$14\frac{1}{4}$	$14\frac{1}{4}$			
	High Gillerthwaite	NY 142141	5	$19\frac{1}{4}$			
	Black Sail Hut	NY 194124	$8\frac{3}{4}$	23			
	X*Honister Pass	NY 225136	$11\frac{1}{4}$	$25\frac{1}{2}$			
	X*Seatoller	NY 244138	13	$27\frac{1}{4}$			
	X*Rosthwaite	NY 259148	$14\frac{1}{2}$	$28\frac{3}{4}$			
	Greenup Edge	NY 286106	$3\frac{3}{4}$	$32\frac{1}{2}$			
	Helm Crag	NY 328092	$7\frac{1}{4}$	36			
	X Grasmere	NY 337075	$9\frac{1}{4}$	38			
	Grisedale Tarn (outlet)	NY 351122	$13\frac{1}{4}$	42			
	X*Patterdale	NY 398159	$17\frac{3}{4}$	$46\frac{1}{2}$			

Angle Tarn (inlet)	NY 417146	2	48½
Kidsty Pike	NY 448126	5	51½
✓ Burnbanks	NY 507161	11	57½
✓ Rosgill Bridge	NY 534165	13¼	59¾
X* Shap	NY 562154	16	62½
✓ Oddendale	NY 593134	2½	65
X* B6260 road	NY 629100	7	69½
✓ Sunbiggin Tarn	NY 677078	11¼	73¾
Smardale Bridge	NY 721059	15½	78
✓ Waitby road	NY 748012	17½	80
X* Kirkby Stephen	NY 774087	20	82½
Nine Standards Rigg	NY 826061	5½	88
✓ Ravenseat	NY 862033	10	92½
X* Keld	NY 892011	12¾	95¼
Swinnergill Mines	NY 912012	1½	96¾
Blakethwaite Mill	NY 937018	3½	98¾
✓ Surrender Bridge	SD 989999	7½	102¾
X* Reeth	SE 038993	11¼	106½

*very infrequent in 2010

LOG OF THE JOURNEY continued

Date	Section	N.G.R.	Miles S	Miles C	Times A	Times D	Weather
	Marrick Priory	SE 067978	2	108½			
✓	Marrick	SE 076982	3	109½			
✓	Marske	NZ 105007	5½	112			
	Whitcliffe Wood	NZ 145014	8½	115			
✗	Richmond	NZ 171009	10½	117			
✗	Colburn	SE 196991	3	120			
✗*	Catterick Bridge	SE 228993	5½	122½			
✓	Bolton-on-Swale	SE 251992	7½	124½			
✓	Kiplin Hall	SE 274977	9½	126¾			
✓	Brockholme	SE 315978	12½	129½			
✓	Danby Wiske	SE 337986	14	131			
✗	Oaktree Hill	SE 361988	16	133			
✓	Long Lane	SE 389998	18½	135¼			
✓	East Harlsey road	NZ 418010	20½	137½			
✗*	A19 road	NZ 442012	22½	139½			
✗	Ingleby Cross	NZ 449007	23	140			

Beacon Hill	SE 460998	$2\frac{1}{2}$	$142\frac{1}{2}$
✓ Huthwaite Green	NZ 492008	$5\frac{1}{2}$	$145\frac{1}{2}$
✓ Carlton Bank	NZ 522030	$8\frac{1}{4}$	$148\frac{1}{4}$
✓* Clay Bank Top	NZ 572033	$12\frac{1}{4}$	$152\frac{1}{4}$
Urra Moor	NZ 595016	2	$154\frac{1}{4}$
Bloworth Crossing	NZ 616015	$3\frac{1}{2}$	$155\frac{3}{4}$
✗† Lion Inn, Blakey	SE 679997	9	$161\frac{1}{4}$
✓ White Cross	NZ 682020	$10\frac{3}{4}$	163
✓ Glaisdale (station)	NZ 783056	$18\frac{3}{4}$	171
✓ Egton Bridge	NZ 804052	2	173
✓ Grosmont	NZ 829052	$3\frac{1}{2}$	$174\frac{1}{2}$
✗ A169 road	NZ 862047	6	177
✓ Littlebeck	NZ 879049	$7\frac{1}{4}$	$178\frac{1}{4}$
✓ Falling Foss	NZ 888035	$8\frac{1}{2}$	$179\frac{1}{2}$
✓ May Beck (car park)	NZ 892024	$9\frac{1}{2}$	$180\frac{1}{2}$
✓ B1416 road	NZ 901041	$10\frac{3}{4}$	$181\frac{3}{4}$
✗ Hawsker	NZ 928074	$14\frac{1}{4}$	$185\frac{3}{4}$
✗ Robin Hood's Bay	NZ 953049	19	190

* very infrequent in 2010

† Moors Bus: spring and summer only

RECORD OF ACCOMMODATION USED ON THE WALK

Provision is made below for 15 beds and breakfasts, which should be more than enough

Date of arrival	Address	Charge

USEFUL INFORMATION

PLANNING AND PREPARATION

The internet is a great resource for those is search of practical information. Some websites have message boards which walkers can use to ask questions or share their experiences of the route. These are good places to start:

www.wainwright.org.uk (the website of The Wainwright Society has a Coast to Coast section with the latest updates).

www.coast2coast.co.uk

www.coasttocoastguides.co.uk

ACCOMMODATION

There is a wide range of accommodation – from guest houses, bed & breakfast, Youth Hostels, bunk-house barns and camping sites – available all along the route. Some helpful pointers below:

A list of bed & breakfast accommodation along the route appears yearly as *The Coast to Coast Bed & Breakfast Accommodation Guide*. The price in 2017 was £6.00 including postage. Apply to Mrs Doreen Whitehead, Kisdon View, Keld, Richmond, North Yorkshire DL11 6LJ. Tel. 01748 886968.

www.yha.org.uk
The Youth Hostels Association (England & Wales) Ltd, Trevelyan House, Dimple Road, Matlock, Derbyshire DE4 3YH
Tel. (reservations) 01629 592700.

BOOKING AND BAGGING SERVICES

Some companies will organise the whole walk for you: work out an itinerary, find and book accommodation and provide a baggage service so that you can enjoy the walk without a heavy backpack. Check the internet for Coast to Coast holiday services – the ones listed here are just a start:

www.c2cpackhorse.co.uk
The Coast to Coast Packhorse
Chestnut House, Crosby Garrett, Kirkby Stephen, Cumbria CA17 4PR
Tel. 01768 371777

www.contours.co.uk
Contours Walking Holidays
Barton House, 21 North End, Wirksworth, Derbyshire DE4 4FG
Tel. 01629 821900

www.macsadventure.com
Macs Adventure Limited
44 Speirs Wharf, Glasgow, Scotland G4 9TH
Tel. 0141 530 8886

www.mickledore.co.uk
Mickledore Travel Ltd
42 St John Street, Keswick, Cumbria CA12 5AG
Tel. 017687 72335

www.sherpavan.com
Sherpa Van Project
29 The Green, Richmond, North Yorkshire DL10 4RG
Tel. 0871 5200124 (baggage); 01609 883731 (accommodation).